Japanese History
11 Experts Reflect on the Past

装幀 ● 菊地信義
装画 ● 野村俊夫

挿画 ● 大森只光

翻訳 ● 浅沼昭子
編集 ● 鈴木節子

Published by Kodansha International Ltd.,
17-14 Otowa 1-chome, Bunkyo-ku, Tokyo 112-8652.
No part of this publication may be reproduced
in any form or by any means without permission
in writing from the publisher.
Copyright © 1996 Kodansha International Ltd.
All rights reserved. Printed in Japan.

First Edition 1996

ISBN4-7700-2024-4
    99 00   20 19 18 17 16

英語で読む日本史
Japanese History
11 Experts Reflect on the Past

「英文日本大事典」[編]

Bilingual **B**ooks

序文

　本書はエンサイクロペディア・オブ・ジャパン（現在、1巻本、英文日本大事典として講談社より刊行中）の中から日本史の各項目に寄稿した諸教授の方を集めて1巻としてまとめたものである。この百科事典の編集に当たっては、項目の選定から執筆者との内容、スタイルにわたり3年以上も費して行なわれたもので、日本史だけに限って言っても、担当執筆者との連絡・統一にも完成には10年余の日時を費した。それだけに、代表的日本史研究家である諸家が心血をそそいで執筆されたもので、通史としてもコンパクトでありながら、日本及び諸外国の研究家の研究業績をくまなく参照し、芸術的にもいささかの遺漏の見られない本となっている。

　しかも、ただ普通の教科書としてだけでなく、寄稿された諸先生方のスタイルが十分に発揮されているので、対訳として日本語と英語を読み比べる楽しみも十分に味わうことができ、かつ日本語を学習する学生にも、英語を学習する学生にも、勉学の大きな助けとなるはずと期待している。

　エンサイクロペディア・オブ・ジャパンの編集について、オーティス・ケリー教授が、この百科事典は、明治以来の日本研究の成果を集大成するもので、将来のジャパノロジーの礎石として大きな貢献をするであろうと予言されたが、本書がその業績の上に立った日本史の通史として多くの読者に愛読されることを期待したい。

創価女子短期大学教授

英文日本大百科事典編集長

板坂　元

Preface

This is a compilation of articles from the Japanese History section of "Kodansha Encyclopedia of Japan." (Now available as one volume under the title of "Japan: An Illustrated Encyclopedia") In compiling the encyclopedia, more than three years were spent selecting the contributors, designing the contents, and choosing an appropriate style. However, coordinating writers for the Japanese history section alone took almost ten years. The writers are representative scholars of Japanese history, all of whom put outstanding effort into the writing of this section. Although a concise general history, it incorporates thorough references to comprehensive research and study in Japan and other countries. It has a unique aesthetic value in that each article clearly reflects the writer's style, giving the reader the pleasure of bilingual appreciation in Japanese and English. I believe this volume will be of great benefit to students of Japanese as well as English, more so than an ordinary textbook.

Professor Otis Cary predicted that "Kodansha Encyclopedia of Japan" would be the most comprehensive work of Japan studies since the Meiji period, making a major contribution to the direction of future studies in Japanology. I anticipate that many people will read this book as a primary source of general Japanese history.

Gen Itasaka

Professor, Soka Women's Junior College
Editor in Chief, "Kodansha Encyclopedia of Japan."

凡例

1873年1月1日の改歴以前の年月日は、太陰暦から太陽歴(西暦)に換算した。太陰暦と太陽歴の年初のずれを考慮して、換算は出来る限り正確に行なった。このため本書における日付は、時として他書と異なるが、それは他書が太陰暦の年初や年末を誤った太陽歴に比定しているためである。

EDITORIAL CONVENTION

Dates prior to Japan's adoption of the Western calendar on 1 January 1873 have been converted from the old Japanese lunar civil calendar. Every effort has been made to give precise conversions, accounting for the discrepancy between the beginning of the year in the lunar calendar and that in the Western solar calendar. Thus the dates given in this book will sometimes differ from those found in many other reference sources, both Japanese and Western, which frequently assign a date at the beginning or end of the lunar year to the wrong solar year.

目次
CONTENTS

CONT

E   N   T   S

執筆者 Writers

ピーター・ブリード　Peter Bleed
　ネブラスカ大学教授。本書「縄文・弥生・古墳時代」執筆。

J. エドワード・キダー, Jr.　J. Edward Kidder Jr.
　元ICU（国際基督教大学）教授。本書「飛鳥時代」執筆。

竹内理三　Takeuchi Rizō
　早稲田大学名誉教授。本書「奈良時代」執筆。

G. カメロン・ハーストIII　G. Cameron Hurst III
　カンザス大学教授。本書「平安時代」執筆。

篠田　稔　Shinoda Minoru
　ハワイ大学教授。本書「鎌倉時代」執筆。

マーティン・C・カルカット　Martin C. Collcutt
　プリンストン大学教授。本書「室町時代」執筆。

ジャージス・エリソーナス　Jurgis Elisonas
　インディアナ大学教授。本書「安土桃山時代」執筆。

ジョン・W・ホール　John W. Hall
　エール大学教授。本書「江戸時代」執筆。

マリウス・B・ジャンセン　Marius B. Jansen
　プリンストン大学教授。本書「明治時代」執筆。

ピーター・ドゥース　Peter Duus
　スタンフォード大学教授。本書「大正時代」執筆。

ピーター・フロスト　Peter Frost
　ウィリアムカレッジ教授。本書「昭和時代」執筆。

英語で読む日本史

Japanese History

縄文時代

（紀元前10,000年ごろ～紀元前300年ごろ）

人々が狩りと採集による生活を営んでいた先史時代の一部で、その名称はこの時代の土器にほどこされた縄目の文様、すなわち縄文に由来する。縄文時代は、土器の存在によりそれ以前の旧石器時代と明確に区分される。縄文時代に続く弥生時代には金属の使用と水稲耕作という特徴が現れる。

縄文草創期（紀元前10,000年ごろ～紀元前7,500年ごろ）は、土器作りの技術と旧石器時代後期の石器作りの技術を併せ持った過渡的な時代である。世界最古の年代の確認された土器は紀元前10,750～10,000年のもので、長崎県福井洞穴など、日本南部の遺跡数か所から発掘されている。

Jōmon pottery
A deep pot featuring the raised–line decorations and extravagant rim ornamentation characteristic of Middle–Jōmon–period kaen pottery.

縄文早期および前期

縄文早期（紀元前7,500年ごろ～紀元前5,000年ごろ）の大きな新しい動きは、海と海岸の資源の活用で、その結果、最初の貝塚が現れる。考古学的な遺跡から発掘される基本的な石器類、竪穴住居址、土偶、縄文式土器などの遺物が伝える縄文文化もこの時代に確立した。貝塚には、この時代の人々が広範な資源を活用していたことを示す証拠が残されている。彼らは魚や貝を採るだけでなく、鹿や猪を狩り、野生の植物の種子など、植物性の食べ物も採取していた。縄文文化はこの時代から、地理的にほぼ東日本の落葉広葉樹林帯と日本列島の西南端の照葉樹林帯に属する2つの文化圏に分かれていた。

Grooved–line geometric patterns decorate this Late–Jōmon–period large deep pot.

Jōmon Period

(ca. 10,000 B.C.–ca. 300 B.C.)

Prehistoric period during which the peoples of Japan followed a hunting and gathering way of life, so called because pottery of this period is decorated with *jōmon* cord-marking. It was preceded by the Paleolithic period, from which it is distinguished by the presence of pottery, and was followed by the Yayoi period, the distinguishing characteristics of which are the use of metals and wet-rice cultivation.

The Incipient Jōmon period (ca. 10,000 B.C.–ca. 7500 B.C.) is a transitional period, marked by the combining of pottery-making with late paleolithic stone-working techniques. The world's oldest known pottery dates from between 10,750 and 10,000 B.C. and was excavated from Fukui Cave in Nagasaki Prefecture and other sites in southern Japan.

INITIAL AND EARLY JŌMON PERIODS

The major innovation of the Initial Jōmon period (ca. 7500 B.C.–ca. 5000 B.C.) was the utilization of marine and coastal resources leading to the accumulation of the first shell mounds. At this time the Jōmon cultural assemblage—including basic stone tools, pit houses, clay figurines, and cord-marked pottery vessels—was also established. The evidence of shell middens indicates that the economy was well rounded: not only were fish and shellfish collected, but deer and wild pigs were hunted and wild seeds and plant foods were gathered. From this time onward, Jōmon culture was divided into two spheres, roughly corresponding to the deciduous forests of eastern Japan and the broadleaf evergreen forests of the southwestern end of the archipelago.

縄文前期（紀元前5,000年ごろ〜紀元前3,500年ごろ）には、気候の温暖化によって海の水位が上がり、沿岸の低地は遠浅の干潟になった。貝殻と魚の骨の堆積である貝塚は、当時の人々が海岸でその資源を採取し、活用していたことを立証している。西日本では、このころから海に出て漁をしていた可能性も考えられる。

縄文中期・後期および晩期

文化の中心は沿岸地域から関東地方の内陸に移り、縄文中期（紀元前3,500年ごろ〜紀元前2,500年ごろ）には、半ば定住型の大きな集落が発達した。火炎土器や土偶はこの時代に現れる。縄文後期（紀元前2,500年ごろ〜紀元前1,000年ごろ）には、東日本の太平洋沿岸で海洋資源の活用がさらに活発化した。人々は多様な道具と技術を開発して、本格的な沖合での漁に乗り出したのである。縄文晩期（紀元前1,000年ごろ〜紀元前300年ごろ）には、進んだ技法の土器が太平洋沿岸の東北地方北部から瀬戸内地方に広まった。土器に見られる技術的な共通性は、縄文晩期には、九州、西日本、朝鮮半島の間に定期的な接触があったことを強く示唆している。

　九州に伝わった稲作と弥生文化の急速な浸透が、縄文時代の生活様式に終止符を打った。

Jōmon figurine
Archaeologists have dubbed this Final-Jōmon-period artifact the "goggle figurine."

High sea levels caused by warm climates during the Early Jōmon period (ca. 5000 B.C.–ca. 3500 B.C.) turned coastal lowlands into tidal marshes, and huge accumulations of seashells and fish bones attest to the exploitation of this resource through coastal gathering. In western Japan, deep-sea fishing may also have been undertaken.

MIDDLE, LATE, AND FINAL JŌMON PERIODS

The center of Jōmon culture gradually shifted from the coasts to the interior of the Kantō district, where large semisedentary villages developed during the Middle Jōmon period (ca. 3500 B.C.–ca. 2500 B.C.). Flamboyantly encrusted pottery and Jōmon figurines appeared during the period. In the Late Jōmon period (ca. 2500 B.C.–ca. 1000 B.C.), a more vigorous marine economy developed along the Pacific coast of eastern Japan. The fishermen of this period invented a vast array of tools and techniques that allowed them to undertake true deep-sea fishing. The Final Jōmon period (ca. 1000 B.C.–ca. 300 B.C.) saw the spread of a series of elaborate pottery styles along the Pacific coast from northern Tōhoku to the Inland Sea region. Similarities in ceramics of the period strongly suggest that there was regular contact between Kyūshū and western Japan and the Korean peninsula during the Final Jōmon period.

The introduction of rice farming to Kyūshū and the rapid spread of Yayoi culture brought an end to the Jōmon lifestyle.

弥生時代

（紀元前300年ごろ～紀元300年ごろ）

Yayoi pottery
Long-necked jar. Late
Yayoi period.

集約的な農業と、青銅器と鉄器の使用が始まった時代で、その名称は1884年東京都文京区弥生町で発掘された特徴のある土器の様式に由来する。水田による稲作の技術、冶金術などの新しい技術は、青銅器時代後期の朝鮮半島から九州へ、徐々に伝わった。水稲耕作は九州から西日本全域に急速に広まり、やがて東北地方にまで普及する。かつて弥生時代は登呂遺跡に見るような、のどかな農村の時代であったと考えられていたが、近年はむしろそれとは対照的に、階級社会が生まれ政治的集団の形成が進んだ、闘争の時代であったという見方が強まっている。

集落

弥生時代前期の村落は、沿岸の低地の湿原の近くに位置していた。湿原を堤防で囲み、排水用の堀を設けて、容易に稲作が行われたのである。やがて食生活の中心は米の収穫になり、従来の狩猟や、野生の植物性の食べ物の採取、貝拾いなどは補助的な手段になって、弥生時代中期には農業の集約化が始まった。灌漑と鉄の刃をつけた農具の発達は水の少ない土地にまで耕地を押し広げ、収穫の増大は人口の爆発的な増加を促した。弥生時代中期の茅葺き屋根の竪穴住居と高床式の穀倉からなる村落は、しばしば全体が深い濠で囲まれている。弥生時代中期から後期には、争乱に備えた高地性集落が一般的になる。

Yayoi Period

(ca. 300 B.C.–ca. A.D. 300)

The first period of intensive agriculture and bronze and iron use, so called because of certain characteristic pottery discovered in the Yayoi section of Bunkyō Ward, Tōkyō, in 1884. Wet-rice technology, metallurgy, and other innovations were introduced piecemeal from the late bronze-age cultures of the Korean peninsula into Kyūshū. From there, wet-rice cultivation spread rapidly throughout western Japan and then gradually into northeastern Japan. In contrast to the earlier view of Yayoi as consisting of peaceful agricultural villages (such as the Toro site), the period is increasingly seen as one of competition and warfare, as trends toward social stratification and polity formation took hold.

SETTLEMENT

Villages in the Early Yayoi period were located near the low coastal marshlands, where rice was easily grown in diked fields with drainage canals. The grain harvest was supplemented by hunting, gathering, and shellfish collecting until the agricultural intensification of the Middle Yayoi period. The development of irrigation systems and iron-edged tools allowed the expansion of cultivation onto drier land, and increased harvests stimulated a massive population explosion. The numerous Middle Yayoi villages of thatched pit houses and raised granaries were often surrounded by substantial village ditches. From the Middle to the Late Yayoi periods, settlements in defensive upland hilltop positions were common.

文化

弥生時代の人々は、縄文時代以来の打製・磨製の石器を使うかたわら、鉄を精錬し、単純な道具を鍛造する方法を知っていた。最初は大陸から渡来した道具が多かったが、弥生時代後期には、青銅の鏡や、銅鐸（どうたく）、青銅の武器などを自らつくるようになっている。彼らは勾玉（まがたま）と呼ばれる湾曲した装飾用の玉を作る技術も開発した。弥生式土器の技法は、大陸から伝わった新しい技術と、頸の長い壺や台付きの鉢（高坏（たかつき））などの形によって、従来の縄文式土器の技法が変化したものである。

　考古学的な遺物は、弥生時代の人々がさまざまな神々のために宗教的な祭礼を行った事実を明らかにしている。死者の埋葬に副葬品を添える習慣もこの時代に発達し、銅鏡、玉飾り、銅剣などが墓地から発掘されている。

国際関係

1784年、福岡県の志賀島（しかのしま）で発見された、漢委奴国王（かんのわのなのこくおう）という金印は、紀元57年、後漢の皇帝が九州北部の小さな「国」の「王」に授けたものと考えられている。

　弥生時代の文化と政治に関する情報は、『魏（ぎ）志』倭人伝（しわじんでん）など、中国の歴代王朝の歴史書に記録されている。当時の日本には国（くに）と呼ばれるかなり複雑な政治単位があり、多くの国が女王卑弥呼（ひみこ）の治める邪馬台国（やまたいこく）の支配下にあったという。吉野ヶ里（よしのがり）遺跡はこれらの記述にある文化を代表する遺跡である。

dōtaku
Elaborately decorated
ceremonial bronze
bells more than 1,600
years old have been
discovered in various
places in Japan.

bronze mirrors
A "flower petals"
mirror excavated
from the Ōtsuka tomb
in Nara Prefecture.
This popular motif
was based on Chinese
models.

CULTURE

Some chipped stone tools of the Jōmon culture continued to be used, but Yayoi people also knew how to smelt iron and forge simple implements. Some items were initially obtained from the continent, but by the Late Yayoi the Japanese themselves were making bronze mirrors, bronze bells (*dōtaku*), and bronze weapons. Techniques were also developed for producing carved jewelry (*magatama*). The Yayoi pottery tradition is a transformation of the Jōmon earthenware tradition with new techniques and shapes (long-necked jars, pedestaled bowls) from the continent.

Archaeological records offer evidence of Yayoi religious festivals honoring various deities. The custom of burying objects with the dead also developed during this period; mirrors, beads, and bronze weapons have been discovered in burial sites.

INTERNATIONAL RELATIONS

A gold seal of the king of the state of Na of Wa of Han was discovered in 1784 on Shikanoshima, in Fukuoka Prefecture. It is believed to have been presented to a "king" in a small northern Kyūshū "country" by the Later Han emperor in A.D. 57.

Information about Yayoi culture and politics was inscribed in the Chinese dynastic histories such as the *Wei zhi* (*Gishi*). Relatively complex political units called *kuni* are recorded, a number under the hegemony of Yamatai, ruled by Queen Himiko. The Yoshinogari site is thought to represent the level of development reflected in these descriptions.

古墳時代

（300〜710年ごろ）

原史時代。地域を支配した豪族の埋葬のために、巨大な墳丘（古墳）が築かれた時代で、前期（4世紀）、中期（5世紀）、後期（6〜7世紀）に分けられる。政治的には飛鳥時代（593〜710）を包含し、日本の最初の国家、大和政権は古墳時代に出現して、朝鮮半島の諸国や中国との間に外交関係を確立した。経済は弥生時代以来の稲作を基礎としながら、5世紀末に、宮廷の必需品の生産に従事する世襲による職業集団、部を中心とした制度に再編された。朝鮮半島の百済から仏教が伝来したのは、6世紀なかば、また、中国の唐にならって大化の改新によって国の統治機構の大改革が行われたのは、7世紀なかばである。

墳丘墓

前期ならびに中期古墳時代の特徴は古墳である。数種類の墳丘が築かれたが、最も特徴的なのは前方後円墳と呼ばれる鍵穴形の古墳である。古墳の多くは埴輪と呼ばれる素焼きの土製品に囲まれている。最大級の5世紀の古墳、仁徳天皇陵と応神天皇陵は大阪府にある。古墳は6世紀になってからも、西日本全域に築かれていた。6世紀なかばに仏教が大陸から伝来すると、権力者はその富を寺院の建立に向けるようになり、やがて仏式の埋葬が主流になる。

Kofun
The largest tomb mound in Japan, said to be that of the emperor Nintoku (early 5th century).

Kofun Period

(ca. 300–710)

Protohistoric period during which large tumuli (*kofun*) were built for deceased members of the ruling elite. The period is divided into three phases: Early (fourth century), Middle (fifth century), and Late (sixth and seventh centuries). It encompasses the Asuka period (593–710). The first state in Japan, Yamato, emerged during the Kofun period, and diplomatic relations were established with the Korean states and the Chinese courts. Based on rice agriculture as established during the Yayoi period, the economy was reorganized in the late fifth century in the form of the *be*, hereditary occupational groups organized to provide the supplies necessary to support palace life. Buddhism was introduced from the kingdom of Paekche on the Korean peninsula in the mid-sixth century, and the state administrative structure was reorganized on the Tang dynasty model through the Taika Reform in the mid-seventh century.

MOUNDED TOMBS

Early and Middle Kofun periods are characterized by *kofun*. Various kinds of mounds were raised, but the most distinct were the "keyhole tombs." Many of the tombs were ringed with *haniwa* (clay objects). The largest fifth-century tombs are the Nintoku and Ōjin mausoleums located in Ōsaka Prefecture. The mounds were built throughout western Japan until well into the sixth century. After the introduction of Buddhism from the continent in the mid-sixth century, the leaders of Japanese society devoted their wealth to the creation of temples, and eventually Buddhist burial patterns came to the fore.

国家の形成

中国の歴史書から知られるように、弥生時代末期の日本には国と呼ばれる小さな政治組織が数多く存在していた。その1つは邪馬台国と呼ばれていたが、この邪馬台国と初期の大和政権とが同一のものであるか、否かは、明らかでない。同時代の中国の記録には、『日本書紀』が伝える天皇の何人かと同一人物を指していると考えられる倭の五王の記述がある。

大和地方およびその周辺には、飾り玉、塩、陶器などをつくっていた大規模な工房の跡が発掘されている。また、地方の豪族の権力の象徴として、重要な意味をもっていた銅鏡についても、その分布調査の結果は大和地方が生産と流通の中心であったことを示している。大和朝廷に物資を納める部の管理が大和地方の豪族の権利と義務になったのは、古墳時代後期である。『古事記』と『日本書紀』の分析的な研究結果は、大和地方の政治的指導者が古墳時代後期に日本を支配したことを示している。

haniwa
Horses are the most common type of animal haniwa.

FORMATION OF THE STATE

It is known from Chinese chronicles that Japan housed many small polities called *kuni* at the end of the Yayoi period. Although one of these was named Yamatai, it is still not known whether Yamatai can be equated with the early state of Yamato. Contemporary Chinese records make mention of the Five Kings of Wa, who may be identifiable with some of the emperors known from the *Nihon shoki* (Chronicle of Japan).

Large manufacturing sites for the production of stone beads, salt, and ceramics have been found in and around the Yamato area; also, distributional studies have shown that the Yamato area was the center for the production and distribution of bronze mirrors, which were important symbolic articles in the regalia of local leaders. Organization of trade to provide goods for the court became a right and responsibility of the Yamato leaders during the Late Kofun period. Analysis of the *Kojiki* (Record of Ancient Matters) and *Nihon shoki* indicates that the political leaders of Yamato became the rulers of the whole country during the Late Kofun period.

飛鳥時代

（593〜710年）

飛鳥時代は593年、女帝推古天皇が大和国飛鳥の豊浦宮（とゆらのみや）で即位した年に始まり、通常、日本の歴史時代の始まりと考えられている。飛鳥時代には、645年、孝徳天皇が都を難波に遷して大化の改新の詔（みことのり）を宣した後の10年間、さらに、694年、女帝持統天皇が都を藤原京に遷してから、710年の平城京への遷都までの期間が含まれる。

仏教と蘇我氏の台頭

飛鳥は蘇我氏の勢力圏にあった。蘇我氏の指導者たちは臣（おみ）の称号、姓（かばね）をもち、大臣となって大和朝廷の財務・外交を掌握し、大陸の文化、とりわけ仏教を日本に移入するうえで、重要な役割を果たした。蘇我氏はまた、天皇家に皇后や妃を立てる権限をもっていた。この権限は後に物部氏（もののべ）と中臣氏（なかとみ）にも与えられる。彼らはいずれも連（むらじ）の姓をもち、物部氏は軍事を担い、中臣氏は神事・祭祀をつかさどった。

　『日本書紀』によれば552年に伝来した仏教（538年の伝来という説もある）の受け入れ問題は、一方を蘇我氏とし、他方を物部氏と中臣氏とする対立と密接に結びついていた。587年、蘇我馬子（そがのうまこ）の率いる蘇我氏は物部守屋（もののべのもりや）を襲い、一族ともども滅ぼして、朝廷における蘇我氏の支配権と仏教の受容を阻む最大の勢力を排除した。

Asuka Period

(593–710)

Period dated from 593, the year in which Empress Suiko was crowned and took up residence in the Toyura Palace in Asuka, Yamato Province. The Asuka period is usually considered to coincide with the beginning of the historic age in Japan. The period also includes the decade after 645, when Emperor Kōtoku removed the capital to Naniwa and issued the edicts of the Taika Reform; and the interval that began in 694 when Empress Jitō entered Fujiwarakyō, and ended in 710 when the capital was shifted to Heijōkyō.

BUDDHISM AND THE ASCENDANCY OF THE SOGA FAMILY

Asuka was the territory of the Soga family, whose leaders possessed the title *omi* and served the Yamato court in the ministerial capacity of financial administrators and diplomats, and were instrumental in introducing continental culture, in particular Buddhism, to Japan. The Soga also held the right to provide consorts and wives to the imperial line. This right was later granted to the Mononobe family and the Nakatomi family, both of which held the title *muraji* and were, respectively, professional soldiers and proprietors of Shintō religious affairs.

The acceptance of Buddhism—reported in the *Nihon shoki* to have been introduced in 552 (another traditional date of introduction is 538)—became closely linked to rivalry between the Soga family on one side and the Mononobe and the Nakatomi on the other. In 587 the Soga, led by Soga no Umako, attacked Mononobe no Moriya, destroying him and his family and thereby clearing the chief opposition to both Soga dominance at court and the acceptance of Buddhism.

初期の寺院と聖徳太子の文化的役割

『日本書紀』によれば、588年、蘇我馬子は日本で初めての、1塔3金堂という完成された伽藍配置をもつ飛鳥寺の建立に着手した。593年、推古天皇は即位と同時に仏教の受容を宣言し、寺院の建立を奨励する。その年、再び『日本書紀』によれば、聖徳太子は四天王寺の建立を命じた。593年に推古天皇の摂政と皇太子に任命された聖徳太子は、605年に斑鳩宮に移り住み、斑鳩寺を建立した。604年、聖徳太子が十七条憲法を制定し、冠位十二階という冠による位階制度を定めたことは、氏姓制度の改革の第一歩となった。

Prince Shōtoku
(574–622). Statesman
of the Asuka period.
As regent for the
empress Suiko, Prince
Shōtoku instituted the
kan'i jūnikai and the
Seventeen-Article
Constitution to
strengthen imperial
authority.

　624年の寺と僧尼の調査報告には、816人の僧と569人の尼僧が住む、46の寺院の記載がある。薬師寺は、後に持統天皇となる天武天皇の皇后が病に臥したときに、天武天皇の命によって建立された。

天皇家の宮殿

『日本書紀』によると、645年から653年にかけて難波京に造営された孝徳天皇の宮城は言葉にならないほど壮大なものであった。随所に中国様式を取り入れていたものと思われる。天武天皇が672年に造営した飛鳥浄御原宮にも、中国式の宮城の特徴的なデザインを多く取り入れている。飛鳥時代には1人の支配者が宮城を1つ、あるいはそれ以上、造営することが慣わしであったために、安定した政治秩序の形成は阻まれた。694年に持統天皇が造営した藤原宮は、文武・元明天皇に引き継がれ、712年まで3代の天

EARLY TEMPLES AND THE CULTURAL ROLE OF PRINCE SHŌTOKU

In 588, according to the *Nihon shoki*, Soga no Umako initiated construction of Asukadera, the first full-fledged *garan*, or temple compound, in Japan. In 593, upon acceding to the throne, Empress Suiko declared her acceptance of Buddhism and encouraged the building of temples. In the same year, again according to the *Nihon shoki*, Prince Shōtoku ordered the construction of Shitennōji. In 605, Shōtoku, who in 593 had been appointed regent and crown prince to Suiko, took up residence in Ikaruga, and at about this time built the temple Ikarugadera. In 604, he issued the Seventeen-Article Constitution and established the court ranks, *kan'i jūnikai* (twelve grades of cap rank)—the first step in the process of replacing the *uji-kabane* system.

A census in 624 lists 46 temples attended by 816 monks and 569 nuns. The construction of Yakushiji was ordered in 680 by Emperor Temmu when his consort, who later reigned as Empress Jitō, fell ill.

IMPERIAL PALACES

The *Nihon shoki* describes the palace of Emperor Kōtoku, built between 645 and 653 in the capital city Naniwakyō, as too magnificent for words. It must have borrowed many elements from the Chinese model. Asuka Kiyomihara no Miya, constructed in 672 by Emperor Temmu, also introduced many features of Chinese palace design. It was the custom during much of the Asuka period for each ruler to build one or more palaces, a practice that inhibited the development of a stable political order. Fujiwara no Miya, occupied between 694 and 710 by Empress Jitō and her successors, Mommu and Gemmei, was the first multigenerational palace.

皇の宮城となった。藤原宮は複数の天皇によっ
て営まれた初めての宮城である。

大化の改新

622年の聖徳太子の死と、626年の蘇我馬子の
死のあと、蘇我氏の指導者たちは皇位継承問題
のからんだ権力闘争で、ますます高圧的な手段
をとるようになる。645年、中臣鎌足（後の藤原鎌
足）と、中大兄皇子（後の天智天皇：在位661〜
672）は、蘇我馬子の孫、蘇我入鹿が暗殺された
クーデターで指導的な役割を果たした。朝廷は
蘇我氏の勢力圏から難波へ移される。646年に
出された四か条の詔は、すでに進行中の改革の
基礎を築き、大化の改新と呼ばれる。四か条の
詔は土地の管理方式と政府の構造を定めたも
ので、その実施には、土地の区画方法の定義
（条里制）、人口調査、税制（租、庸、調）の賦課、
耕作能力をもつ家族と個人への土地の割り当て
（班田収授の法）が必要であった。8省からなる
官職と、貴族のための新しい冠位十九階も、649
年までに制定されている。

天智天皇・天武天皇の治世

大化の改新後の日本の国内の安定を脅かした
のは、新羅である。大和朝廷は、新羅とその強
力な連合国、中国の唐に対抗して、日本と緊密
な関係にある百済を守るために、朝鮮半島に援
軍を送った。663年、日本・百済連合軍が唐軍と
の決定的な海戦（白村江の戦い）に破れ、百済
が滅びたのは、天智天皇の治世でのことである。
　天智天皇は672年に没し、彼が望んだ後継者、
その皇子である大友皇子を壬申の乱で打ち負

THE TAIKA REFORM

Following the deaths of Prince Shōtoku in 622 and Soga no Umako in 626, manipulation by Soga family leaders in succession struggles became increasingly high-handed. In 645, Nakatomi no Kamatari (later Fujiwara no Kamatari) and Prince Naka no Ōe (later to rule as Emperor Tenji from 661 to 672) played leading roles in a coup in which Soga no Iruka, grandson of Umako, was assassinated. The court was removed from Soga territory to Naniwa. Four edicts issued in 646 laid the basis for an ongoing process of reform; they are known as the Taika Reform. They dealt with land control and government structure. The implementation of the edicts required the definition of land boundaries (*jōri* system), a census, the levying of taxes (*so, yō,* and, *chō*), and allotment of land to families and individuals responsible for cultivation (*handen shūju* system). By 649, eight state ministries and a new system of nineteen ranks for the nobility had been established.

THE REIGNS OF EMPERORS TENJI AND TEMMU

Domestic security in the wake of the Taika Reform was threatened by Silla. A Japanese expedition was sent to the Korean peninsula to defend Paekche, with which Japan had close ties, against Silla and its powerful ally, Tang China. In 663, during the reign of the emperor Tenji, Japan was defeated in a decisive naval engagement with the Tang (the Battle of Hakusonkō), and Paekche was vanquished.

Emperor Tenji expired in 672. His son Prince Ōtomo, the preferred successor, was defeated in the Jinshin Disturbance

かした天智天皇の弟は、天武天皇として、地方
および中央の官人の登用制度の改革を推し進
めた。684年には八色の姓を定め、689年に飛鳥
浄御原令として公布される律令の編纂に着手し
た。飛鳥浄御原令は、刑法（律）と行政規定（令）
に分かれた日本で最初の法典で、701年に制定
された、より包括的な大宝律令の基礎になって
いる。

文化

飛鳥時代は文化的に、仏教の影響の強い、韓
国からの渡来人がもたらした中国文化の同化の
時代である。渡来人は僧侶、寺院建築の技術
者、瓦工など、多くの分野の専門家であった。
彼らはまた、儒教の古典、大陸の音楽や舞踊、
中国の宮廷の儀式などを伝えている。飛鳥時代
後期に発達した文化は白鳳文化と呼ばれる。

Chūgūji
This convent-temple's
main icon, the Asuka-
period lacquer-on-
wood image of the
bodhisattva Miroku,
shown here, has been
designated a National
Treasure.

　現存する飛鳥時代の美術品は、ほとんど全て、
仏教の信仰と関連がある。仏師鞍作止利による
法隆寺の釈迦三尊像は、北魏様式の影響の強
い作品で、早期の仏像である。ほかに、ほぼ同
時代の重要な作品として、中宮寺の弥勒菩薩
半跏思惟像がある。7世紀の絵画の代表的な例
としては、玉虫厨子の鏡板には釈迦の前世が描
かれている。白鳳文化の顕著な例は、薬師寺東
塔と当麻寺弥勒菩薩像である。

The 7th-century **Kudara Kannon** is
a bodhisttva carved from a block of
comphor wood. Its name links it to
Kudara (Paekche).

by Tenji's brother, who became Emperor Temmu. He made further reforms in the system of hiring provincial and central government bureaucrats, established a new system of eight honorary cognomens (*yakusa no kabane*) in 684, and initiated the compilation of legal statutes that were distributed in 689 as the Asuka Kiyomihara Code. This was the first Japanese legal code to be divided into criminal laws (*ritsu*) and administrative regulations (*ryō*), and it formed the basis for the more comprehensive Taihō Code of 701.

CULTURE

Strongly influenced by Buddhism, the culture of the Asuka period represented an assimilation of the Chinese culture transmitted to Japan by Korean immigrants (*toraijin*). They were specialists in a number of fields, including among them priests, temple builders, and roof-tile makers; they also introduced the Confucian classics, continental music and dance, and Chinese court ceremonies. The culture developed late in the Asuka period is called the Hakuhō culture.

Almost all of the works of art that remain from the Asuka period are related to Buddhist worship. The Shaka Triad (623) at Hōryūji by Kuratsukuri no Tori, a work that is strongly influenced by the Northern Wei sculptural style, is an early piece of Buddhist statuary. Another important piece from about the same time is the seated Miroku Buddha at Chūgūji. A significant example of painting from the mid-seventh century is found at the Tamamushi Shrine, on whose panels are depicted scenes from the previous lives of the Buddha. Outstanding examples of the Hakuhō culture are the east pagoda of Yakushiji and the Miroku Buddha at Taimadera.

奈良時代

（710〜794年）

都が大和の平城京（現在の奈良）に置かれた時代。奈良時代は、都が藤原京から平城京に遷された710年に始まり、784年の長岡京への遷都で終わる。しかし、奈良時代は通常、長岡京に都のあった10年間を含めて、710年から794年とされる。奈良時代の特徴は、律令制の全面的な実施、朝廷の宗教として、したがって国教としての仏教の確立、東大寺大仏殿の造営によって示される、かつてない高水準に達した知識と文化にある。しかし、土地保有制度の修正と、重税に耐えかねた農民の公有地からの逃亡は、中央集権制度の崩壊につながった。

政治的発展

奈良時代の政治は、藤原氏と、それに対抗する橘氏、大伴氏などと不満を抱く皇族の間の、一連の権力闘争とみなされる。奈良時代初期に朝廷で指導的な地位にあったのは藤原不比等である。

不比等が720年に没した後、朝廷で最大の権力を握ったのは長屋王であるが、彼は729年、謀反を企てたとして、天皇に自害を命じられた（長屋王の変）。それは、実際には藤原氏の陰謀で、長屋王は無実であるといわれる。しかし、737年、不比等の息子4人全員の天然痘による死が、藤原氏の皇位への野望に終止符を打った。

Nara Period

(710–794)

The period during which the seat of government was at Heijōkyō (now Nara) in Yamato. The Nara period proper began in 710, when the imperial capital was moved from Fujiwarakyō, and ended in 784 with the transfer of the capital to Nagaokakyō. Dates for the period are usually given as 710–794, however, to include the ten years during which the capital was in Nagaoka. The period was characterized by the full implementation of the *ritsuryō* system of government; the establishment of Buddhism as the religion of the court and, by extension, of the state; and new heights in intellectual and cultural achievement, as exemplified by the building of the Great Hall of the temple Tōdaiji. Modifications in the land tenure system, and the absconding from state lands of peasants overburdened by taxes, contributed to the breakdown of central authority.

POLITICAL DEVELOPMENTS

The political history of the Nara period may be seen as a series of struggles for power that pitted the Fujiwara family against factions composed of, among others, members of the Tachibana and Ōtomo families, in association with disaffected members of the imperial family.

The leader of the government at the beginning of the Nara period was Fujiwara no Fuhito. Following the death of Fuhito in 720, the most powerful political figure was Prince Nagaya, but in 729 the prince was ordered by the emperor to commit suicide for allegedly fomenting a rebellion (Rebellion of Nagaya no Ō). He had, in fact, been falsely accused by members of the Fujiwara family. The death of all four of

　不比等の娘光明子を皇后としていた聖武天皇
は、このような事態に深く心を傷め、仏の力で疫
病や社会不安を鎮めることを期待して、741年、
全国に僧寺と尼寺の建立（国分寺創建）を命じ、
743年には東大寺の大仏の造立を命じる。

The huge bronze
statue known as the
Nara Daibutsu. A
representation of the
Buddha Birushana, the
15-meter-high statue,
has been severely
damaged and restored
several times since its
creation in 752.

　749年、聖武天皇が譲位し、娘の孝謙天皇が
即位すると、光明皇太后のために紫微中台が新
設され、藤原仲麻呂がその長官として、政治の
表舞台に姿を現す。彼は親孝行を奨励して、官
位や官職名を中国式に改め、大宝律令（701年）
と養老律令（718年）を編纂した祖父不比等の功
績を顕彰して、757年、遅ればせながら、後者を
施行する。こうして仏教に支配されていた朝廷
が儒教色を帯びるようになる。

　孝謙天皇は退位したが、762年頃には、譲位
した淳仁天皇を支配するようになり、仲麻呂の新
政策に不満を示し、仲麻呂を排して、道鏡禅師
を寵愛する。764年、仲麻呂は反乱を起こすが、
捕らえられ、斬首される。道鏡は太政大臣禅師
に任じられ、法王の称号を与えられる。道鏡の
一党は法参議に任じられ、政権は法王宮職に独
占される。道鏡はついには皇位につこうとする
が、その野望は藤原百川、和気清麻呂らに阻ま
れる。女帝称徳天皇（孝謙上皇は764年、ふた
たび皇位について、称徳と名乗った）は、770年、

Fuhito's sons in a smallpox epidemic in 737, however, put an end to the family's imperial aspirations.

Emperor Shōmu, who was married to Empress Kōmyō, a daughter of Fuhito, was deeply disturbed by this course of events, and, in the hope that the powers of Buddha would bring an end to epidemic disease and social ills, in 741 he ordered the construction of temples and nunneries (*kokubunji*) in every province. In 743 he initiated the construction of the Great Buddha of Tōdaiji.

Emperor Shōmu abdicated in 749 and was replaced by his daughter Empress Kōken. An office (Shibichūdai) was established for the Empress Dowager Kōmyō, and Fujiwara no Nakamaro appeared in the political arena as administrator of her palace affairs. He encouraged the observance of filial piety and renamed official ranks and ministries in the Chinese manner. He publicly commended his grandfather Fuhito for his work in drawing up the Taihō Code (701) and the Yōrō Code (718), and he belatedly enforced the latter from 757. The government, which had hitherto been dominated by Buddhism, now took on a more Confucian aspect.

Although Empress Kōken abdicated from the throne, by 762 she had gained ascendancy over her successor, Emperor Junnin. Displeased with the new measures, she dismissed Nakamaro and instead relied heavily on the priest Dōkyō. In 764 Nakamaro instigated a rebellion but was captured and killed. Dōkyō was elevated to the rank of *dajō daijin zenji* and given the title of *hōō*. With the appointment of his fellow monks as religious councillors (*hōsangi*), court politics was monopolized by the Buddhist clergy. Finally, Dōkyō tried to have himself enthroned but was thwarted by Fujiwara no Momokawa, Wake no Kiyomaro, and others. Empress Shōtoku (the name taken by Empress Kōken when she reascended the throne in

皇位継承者を定めず没し、道鏡は追放された。

　称徳天皇の没後、天智天皇の孫、62歳の白
壁王が光仁天皇として即位する。光仁天皇は財
政の緊縮、役人や僧侶の規律の励行、農村の
再建などに努めるが、中央政府の権威の衰微を
遥かな東北地方で感じとった蝦夷が反乱を起こ
す。反乱は他の地方にも広がり、その鎮圧は長
年の重大課題になる。781年、光仁天皇の皇太
子が桓武天皇として即位し、桓武天皇は794年
の平安遷都を推進した。

社会と経済

奈良時代の社会構造は、大宝律令に示された
律令制度に沿っていた。中央政府の頂点に太
政官があり、国家は国に分割され、国はさらに
郡、郷、里に分割されていた。奈良時代初期の
記録には、67国、555郡、4,012郷、12,036里が列
記されている。各国の統治には、都から派遣さ
れた国司があたり、人民は全て、天皇の臣下と
考えられていた。

　田はすべて公地とされ、班田収授制度のもと
で、6年ごとに、6歳以上の男女全てに再配分さ
れた。当時の人口は500万から600万人、田は
601,000町あったと推定される。田の割り当て
（口分田）を受けた者には、労役（雑徭）、年貢米
（租）、それに手工芸品あるいは地域の特産品
（調）の税が課された。そのほかに、労役の代わ
りに手工芸品もしくは地域の特産品を納める税
（庸）もあった。中央政府は、地方との行政上な

764) died without issue in 770, and Dōkyō was banished.

After the death of Shōtoku, the grandson of Emperor Tenji, 62-year-old Prince Shirakabe, was installed as Emperor Kōnin. His rule was distinguished by efforts to reduce national expenditures, to discipline officials and monks, and to rebuild farming villages. But the decay of the central government's authority was felt as far away as northeastern Japan, where the Ezo tribes rose in rebellion. The rebellion spread to other areas and posed a grave problem for years afterward. In 781 Emperor Kōnin's crown prince acceded to the throne as Emperor Kammu, and it was he who was instrumental in moving the capital to Heiankyō in 794.

SOCIETY AND ECONOMY

The social structure in the Nara period conformed to the *ritsuryō* system, as set forth in the Taihō Code. The central government was headed by the Dajōkan (Great Council of State), and the country was divided into provinces (*kuni* or *koku*), which in turn were divided into districts (*gun*), villages (*gō*), and hamlets (*ri*). An early Nara-period document lists 67 provinces, comprising 555 districts, 4,012 villages, and 12,036 hamlets. The provinces were administered by governors (*kokushi*), who were sent out from the capital. All the people were considered the emperor's subjects.

All rice land was declared public domain. Under the *handen shūju* system (land allotment system), the land was redistributed every six years to all males and females over six years of age. The population is estimated to have been between 5 and 6 million and the acreage of rice land about 601,000 *chō*. Holders of allotted rice land (*kubunden*) were liable to corvée (*zōyō*), a rice tax (*so*), and a handicraft or local products tax (*chō*). There was also a handicraft or local products tax (*yō*) in lieu of labor. To strengthen administra-

らびに軍事上の連携を強め、納税の便宜をはかるために、都と地方政庁所在地を結ぶ幹線道路に駅を置く制度（駅制）を確立する。これによって地域の首長に納められていた税は、直接中央へ送られた。

　それと同時に、歳入を増やす手段として、開墾によって耕地を広げることが奨励された。皇族、貴族、大寺院、地域の権力者、それに小規模ながら農民自身は、8世紀の初めから未開拓地の開墾に取り組んでいる。

　723年、朝廷は三世一身法（さんぜいっしんのほう）を公布した。墾田の私有を3世代まで認めるが、その後は公地として取り上げて、班田制度に組み入れることを定めたのである。しかし、この法律の効果はあがらず、743年には、墾田永年私財法（こんでんえいねんしざいほう）によって、開墾地の永久私有を認めることになった。その結果、貴族階級、大寺院、それに地方の権力者は当然ながら、開墾に努力する。こうして、多くの農民が律令制度の枠外に組織され、土地開発の労働力となった事実は、奈良時代以降の社会の変遷の決定的な要因になった。それが荘園（しょうえん）形成の基礎になった。

天平文化と遣唐使

729〜749年の年号にちなんで呼ばれる天平文化の開花は、中国の唐との関係回復に負うところが少なくない。中国に公式の使節を送ることは、663年、日本軍が白村江（はくそんこう）の戦いに破れて以来途絶えていた。遣唐使を送る決定が下された

tive and military communications with the provinces and to facilitate the payment of taxes, the government established a network of post stations (*ekisei*) on the public roads connecting the capital and provincial seats of government. The rice and produce taxes that had hitherto been paid to local chieftains were now sent directly to the central government.

At the same time, as a means of increasing revenue, there was demand for an expansion of acreage under cultivation through the reclamation of land. Since the early eighth century, members of the royal family, the aristocracy, the great temples, local magnates, and, to a lesser extent, the peasants themselves had set about gaining control of uncultivated lands.

In 723 the government issued the Sanze Isshin no Hō (Law of Three Generations or a Lifetime), a law declaring that reclaimed lands could be held in private hands for up to three generations, but that thenceforth they must be given over to the *handen* system. This law proved to be ineffective, however, and in 743, through the Konden Einen Shizai Hō, the government permitted the privatization of reclaimed lands in perpetuity. As a consequence the aristocracy, great temples, and local magnates redoubled their efforts to reclaim land. The fact that a large number of peasants were thus organized outside of the *ritsuryō* system into a labor force to develop land was a decisive factor in the evolution of society during and after the Nara period, for it created the basis for the formation of privately owned estates (*shōen*).

TEMPYŌ CULTURE AND EMBASSIES TO TANG CHINA

The ripening of Tempyō culture, so termed after the era name (*nengō*) for the years 729–749, was due in no small measure to the resumption of relations with Tang China. The sending of official envoys had been halted since the defeat of Japanese forces in the Battle of Hakusonkō in 663.

のは701年、その一行が出発したのは翌年である。遣唐使は毎回500人から600人の随員とともに、701年から777年の間に7回派遣された。

　中国への旅は、危険で、しばしば命がけの航海だった。その航海に取り組んだことは、中国から学ぼうとした日本人の意欲をうかがわせる。遣唐使には多くの学生や学者が随行し、そのなかには中国に長年留まった者も多い。そしてある者は外国の高僧を招聘し、新しい仏教をもたらした。彼らの全員が天平文化の豊かさのために少なからぬ貢献をした。有名な留学生としては、玄昉（げんぼう）、吉備真備（きびのまきび）、阿倍仲麻呂（あべのなかまろ）などがあげられる。玄昉は経典5,000巻余りを持ち帰り、吉備真備は儒学、軍事学、儀式などを学んで、将来の廷臣のための教育プログラムを作成した。唐の高僧鑑真（がんじん）は日本への渡航を試みて5回失敗したあと、756年、ついに日本に到着する。彼は律宗の教えを伝え、唐招提寺を創建した。

Ganjin (688–763).

　外国人は遠く中央アジアや西アジアから訪れ、天平文化に活気と多様性を添えた。奈良時代の芸術の真髄は正倉院に保存された数千点の宝物に見ることができる。矛盾するように聞こえるかもしれないが、奈良時代の文化は国際色豊かでありながらも、日本独自の文化である。中国の文字は受け入れられたが、日本語はそのまま残った。しかも日本人は中国の漢字を自由に、独創的に用いることによって、日本語を豊かで、微妙な表現の可能な言語に発達させている。歌集『万葉集』はこの時代の最高傑作である。日本の最初の歴史書『古事記』は712年に完成し、

In 701 it was decided to send an embassy to China, and the envoys set out for the continent the following year. Between 701 and 777, seven missions were dispatched, each comprising as many as 500 or 600 men.

The voyages across the sea were perilous and often fatal; that they were undertaken at all indicates the eagerness with which the Japanese sought to learn from China. Many students and scholars accompanied these embassies, a number remaining in China for many years. Some of them brought back foreign monks and new forms of Buddhism; in all, they contributed significantly to the abundance of Tempyō culture. Gembō, Kibi no Makibi, and Abe no Nakamaro are some of the more famous of these students. Gembō returned with more than 5,000 sutras, while Kibi no Makibi, who had studied Confucianism, military science, and ceremonial rites, set up an educational program for future government officials. The Chinese monk Ganjin finally reached Japan in 756 after five unsuccessful attempts. He conveyed the teachings of the Ritsu sect and founded the Tōshōdaiji temple.

Other visitors coming from as far away as Central and West Asia added to the vigor and diversity of Tempyō culture. The quintessence of Nara art is represented in the thousands of objects preserved in the Shōsōin. Contradictory though it may seem, with the extent of foreign influence, the culture of the period remained uniquely Japanese. The Chinese writing system was adopted, but the Japanese language remained intact. Furthermore, by using Chinese characters in a free and imaginative manner, the Japanese added greatly to the richness and subtlety of their language. The poetic anthology *Man'yōshu* (Collection of Ten Thousand Leaves) is an outstanding masterpiece of the period. Japan's first history, the *Kojiki*, was completed in 712; it was followed eight

その8年後に、もう1つ、漢文で書かれた編年体
の歴史書『日本書紀』が完成した。地域の風習、
地勢、産物などを述べた地誌『風土記』も同じこ
ろに編纂されている。

　日本の文学と美術は、大部分が国家の庇護
のもと奈良時代に初めて開花し、平安時代の国
風文化の基礎を築いた。

years later by another chronicle, the *Nihon shoki*, which was written in Chinese (*kambun*). The *fudoki*, gazetteers that described local customs, topography, and products, were compiled around the same time.

The Nara period marked the culmination of the first great flowering of Japanese literature and the fine arts, largely through state sponsorship that laid the foundation upon which the pervasive domestication of continental culture was achieved in the succeeding Heian period.

平安時代

（794〜1185年）

　　平安時代は794年、桓武天皇が平安京（現
　　在の京都）に都を遷してから、1185年、源
頼朝の軍勢が平氏を打ち破って、鎌倉幕府設
立の舞台を整えるまでの、約400年近い期間で
ある。

　日本は平安時代に中国社会の基本要素を完
全に同化し、経済、政治、それに文化の面で、
日本固有の社会制度を創設した。

政治と政治体制

平安時代の政治の変遷は4段階に分けることが
できる。9世紀の初期に終わる第1段階は、政府
の機構改革と軍事活動によって律令制度の活気
を取り戻そうとした、桓武天皇の刷新の時代で
ある。その事業は嵯峨天皇に受け継がれ、政治
の効率を高めるために、律令制度の枠外に、新
たな役所が設置された。しかし、これらの役所
は皇族以外の貴族、とりわけ藤原氏が権力を握
るために利用されるようになる。藤原氏は巧妙
に仕組んだ朝廷での陰謀によって多くの政敵を
排除し、摂政あるいは関白として天皇家に近づ
いた。

　第2段階の9世紀後期から967年までは、藤原
氏の「支援」を受けないで統治した、宇多天皇、
醍醐天皇、村上天皇のもとで、天皇家が藤原氏
の台頭にもかかわらず、その力と権威を維持し
た時代である。しかし朝廷はこの時期に、政治

Heian Period

(794–1185)

The Heian period is a span of nearly 400 years extending from 794, when Emperor Kammu established Heiankyō (now Kyōto) as the imperial capital of Japan, to 1185, when Minamoto no Yoritomo's forces defeated those of the Taira family, thus setting the stage for the establishment of the Kamakura shogunate.

During Heian times, Japan fully assimilated the essence of Chinese society and created indigenous institutions in economics, government, and cultural style.

POLITICS AND GOVERNMENT

The political history of Heian Japan can be divided into a four-phase scheme. In the first phase, which ended in the early ninth century, Kammu attempted to reinvigorate the *ritsuryō* system through various governmental reforms and military campaigns. His work was carried on by Emperor Saga, who created certain extrastatutory offices outside the *ritsuryō* system to enhance government efficiency. These offices, however, created avenues to power for nonimperial royal families, most important among them being the Fujiwara family. Through skillful political maneuvering in several plots at court, the Fujiwara eliminated a number of rival families and drew close to the imperial house as regents (*sesshō* or *kampaku*).

In the second phase, from the late ninth century until 967, the imperial house managed to preserve power and authority in the face of the rise of the Fujiwara under Emperors Uda, Daigo, and Murakami, all of whom ruled without Fujiwara "assistance." But the court faced both political

と財政の両面で、問題に直面する。醍醐天皇は荘園の整理と、地方政府の機構ならびに税制の改革によって、問題を解決しようとした。しかし、地方の豪族は中央の貴族や寺社と結合して荘園を設立、その結果、朝廷による土地と人民の支配は弱まった。

第3段階は、藤原実頼が20年ぶりの摂政に就任した967年に始まる。それからの1世紀は藤原氏による摂関政治の時代で、藤原氏北家は摂関家としての地位を確立した。天皇は藤原氏を母として生まれ、母の実家で養育され、伯父、義父、あるいは祖父の支配下にあった。4人の娘を天皇の后にし、3人の天皇の祖父になった藤原道長と、その息子で、52年間摂政・関白の座を占めた藤原頼道の2人の時代が摂関政治の全盛期である。

平安時代の第4段階は、1世紀ぶりに、藤原氏ではない母親から生まれた天皇、後三条天皇が即位した1068年に始まったと考えられている。この段階が院政時代と呼ばれるのは、3人の譲位して出家した天皇（白河、鳥羽、後白川法皇）が後三条天皇によって創設された天皇家のための私的な権力基盤を活用し、発展させて、天皇や摂政・関白に代わって、平安京の政界で最高の実力者になったからである。

第4段階は天皇家の復権の時代である。天皇家はもはや藤原氏の支配下にあった時のような単なる主権の拠りどころではなくなった。朝廷の支配権を取り戻し、貴族や武家をその庇護下におく強力な一族として、藤原氏をはじめ他の貴族たちと荘園の獲得を競ったのである。

and fiscal problems at this juncture. Daigo tried to solve the matter by regulating *shōen* (landed estates) and reforming provincial government and tax collection. But his efforts were in vain, as court control of land and people continued to be weakened by the collaboration of local landholders with central nobles and religious institutions to create *shōen*.

The third phase is dated from 967, when Fujiwara no Saneyori became regent after a hiatus of twenty years. The next century was the period of Fujiwara regency politics (*sekkan seiji*), when the northern branch of the Fujiwara family established a permanent regency. Emperors were born of Fujiwara mothers and dominated by uncles, fathers-in-law, or grandfathers, in whose households they usually were raised. The two greatest Fujiwara regents were Fujiwara no Michinaga, father of four daughters married to emperors and grandfather of three emperors, and his son Fujiwara no Yorimichi, who held the post of regent for fifty-two years.

The fourth phase of the Heian period is recognized as commencing when Go-Sanjō, the first emperor in a century who had not been born of a Fujiwara mother, came to the throne in 1068. It is called the phase of *insei*, or rule by "cloistered emperor," so named because three successive retired emperors—Shirakawa, Toba, and Go-Shirakawa—replaced emperors and also regents as the supreme political figures at Heiankyō, fully utilizing and expanding upon the private base of power for the imperial house created by Go-Sanjō.

This was a period of revival for the emperors, as the imperial house, no longer simply the repository of sovereignty as it had been under Fujiwara domination, regained control over the imperial position, reorganized itself into a strong private house with aristocratic and military clients, and competed with the Fujiwara and others for *shōen* acquisition.

とはいえ、地域の有力者たちが結託して国家による土地の支配を脅かし、寺院が相互に、また朝廷と争い、社会の法と秩序が崩壊した結果、律令制度は事実上この段階で消滅する。台頭しつつあった武士階級は、保元の乱（1156年）や平治の乱（1160年）によって示されるように、平安京においてさえ、文官による政治体制を維持するために、ますます必要とされるようになった。武家出身の平清盛が朝廷であまりにも高位についたために、平安時代の第5段階として、1160年から1185年までの武家平氏が支配した時代の存在を主張する学者もいる。

Taira no Kiyomori
(1118–81). Prominent
political figure of the
late Heian period. Of
warrior origin, he rose
to dominate the court
and saw his grandson
become emperor.

土地保有制度

743年の墾田永年私財法は、寺院や貴族による大規模な土地の私有を認めたもので、律令制度の精神に反するとはいえ、朝廷は自らの利益のために支持した。9世紀には、開墾、買収、放棄された土地の占有、あるいは臣下に領地として与えることによって獲得された貴族の土地が拡大する。そして、その多くが荘園の形態をとったために、902年、その増大を阻止するために延喜の荘園整理令が発布されるが、この措置は天皇家の私有地を縮小したに過ぎなかった。

公地以外の土地の大部分は荘園であり、11世紀から12世紀、荘園は著しく拡大した。平安時代の末には水田の半分以上が荘園内に組み込まれていた。その結果、貴族階級は減少する公的な収入の埋め合わせに、以前にも増して私有地を求めなければならなかった。公田の制度は鎌倉時代まで存続したが、国家による人民と土

The *ritsuryō* system virtually disappeared during this phase, however, as cliques of powerful local leaders threatened state control over lands, Buddhist institutions quarreled with each other and with the court, and public law and order broke down. The rising military class became increasingly necessary to maintain civil government even in Heiankyō, as demonstrated by the Hōgen Disturbance (1156) and the Heiji Disturbance (1160). One warrior-courtier, Taira no Kiyomori, rose so high in court rank that some scholars postulate the existence of yet a fifth phase of the Heian period, one of Taira warrior domination, from 1160 to 1185.

LANDHOLDING SYSTEM

The Konden Einen Shizai Hō of 743 paved the way for extensive private land ownership by temples and nobles, a movement counter to the spirit of the *ritsuryō* system but supported by government officials who found it profitable. In the ninth century, noble lands, acquired through reclamation, purchase, occupation of abandoned fields, or being placed into vassalage, expanded. Many of these were in the form of *shōen*, and in 902 the Engi Reform was promulgated to stop their growth, but it succeeded only in curtailing the lands of the imperial house.

Nonpublic lands were mostly *shōen*, and their growth over the eleventh and twelfth centuries was so great that, by the end of the Heian period, more than half the total paddy fields were within *shōen*, forcing the nobility to look for ever more private land to replace declining public revenues. Although *kōden* ("public lands") survived well into the Kamakura period, the *ritsuryō* ideal of national control

地の支配という律令国家の理想は、12世紀末に
は久しく失われていたのである。

宗教

仏教の不必要な影響を逃れることも、平安遷都
の理由の1つであったが、桓武天皇をはじめその
の後継者たちは、仏教を敵視したわけではなか
った。仏教は平安時代にも栄え、土着の神道の
信仰と結びついて、貴族階級の宗教と哲学を支
配した。

　平安朝には、中国に留学した2人の僧によっ
て新しい仏教がもたらされた。最澄は比叡山延
暦寺を創建して、天台宗を起こし、真に国家の
ために奉仕する僧団の創設に一身を捧げた。現
に、日本のその後の宗教的指導者の多くは、天
台宗の総本山延暦寺の出身である。延暦寺は、
悪霊の侵入経路と信じられていた、最も危険な
北東に位置するために、やがて都を守護すると
考えられるようになる。

　空海はむしろ弘法大師という諡で知られ、中
国から帰国後、高野山にその寺院を創建した。
空海はタントラ仏教（密教）を真言宗として日本
に伝えている。真言宗は、儀式、加持祈禱、仏
教的宇宙観を視覚化した曼荼羅と呼ばれる整
然とした図像の力強い提示に重点を置いたため
に、朝廷で高い人気を集めた。さらに、空海自
身の才能と強い性格も、貴族階級のあいだに、
密教的要素の濃い真言宗が天台宗よりも強い影
響力を及ぼす原因になっている。

　新しい宗派の仏教の本山は、僧侶のマイナス
の影響力を避けたいという桓武天皇の願いを反
映して、都の外に置かれたが、平安時代中期から

over people and land was long dead by the end of the twelfth century.

RELIGION

Although escaping the undue influence of Buddhism was one of the reasons for removing the capital to Heiankyō, Emperor Kammu and his successors were not hostile to Buddhism. Buddhism flourished in Heian times, and in combination with native Shintō beliefs it dominated the religious and philosophical lives of the nobility.

New forms of Buddhism were brought to the Heian court by two monks who had gone to China. Saichō, who had founded the temple of Enryakuji on Mt. Hiei, established the Tendai sect, dedicating himself to creating a monastic order that would truly serve the nation. Indeed, a large number of Japan's subsequent religious leaders came from the Tendai headquarters at Enryakuji. Situated outside Heiankyō in the critically dangerous northeast, from where it was believed evil spirits invaded, Enryakuji came to be regarded as the protector of the capital.

Kūkai, better known by his posthumous name Kōbō Daishi, returned to found his temple on Mt. Kōya. Kūkai introduced tantric Buddhism into Japan in the form of the Shingon sect. Because it emphasized rituals, incantations, and powerful visual representations of the Buddhist cosmology in cosmic diagrams called *mandala*, Shingon Buddhism proved immensely popular with the Japanese court. Furthermore, Kūkai's own talents and strength of character helped to make esoteric Shingon more influential than Tendai among the nobility.

The headquarters of the new sects of Buddhism were located outside the capital, reflecting Kammu's desire to avoid the negative influence of priests. But from mid-Heian times,

は、貴族が多くの私的な寺院を都に建立している。

　大寺院は、内部あるいは寺院間の激しい教義上の抗争、また荘園の所有に関する紛争の際の守備を担う僧兵を雇用した。宗教と政治の分離は、ときおり危うくなりながらも維持された。しかし、朝廷の貴族たちは常に信心深く、天皇でさえ、名のある神社や寺院にたびたび参詣することが珍しくなかった。

　浄土宗の教義は9世紀に円仁（えんにん）によって中国から伝えられ、空也（くうや）によって広がった。平安時代の浄土信仰の発達に最も重要な役割を果たした人物は源信（げんしん）である。彼は『往生要集（おうじょうようしゅう）』のなかで、地獄の恐ろしさと浄土の喜びを克明に描いている。

　浄土信仰は平安中期以降大きな人気を集めた。上流貴族は阿弥陀如来の導きによる浄土への往生を願って、熱心に念仏を唱え、あるいは信仰の証として、屋敷内に阿弥陀堂を建立した。そのような私的な阿弥陀堂の最も有名な例は、平等院鳳凰堂（びょうどういんほうおうどう）である。

文学

文学の分野は、平安時代の創造的精神の高まりを象徴的に示している。平安時代の文学史の便宜上の、心理的な区分点は、他の分野と同じく、最後の遣唐使が派遣された838年である。

　文学的創造性の飛躍を可能にしたのは、仮名文字の成立である。漢字を一切使わないで日本語の文章を書くことも、理論上は可能になった。しかし、平安時代の廷臣は知識人として中国語の書き言葉（漢文）にこだわり続け、仮名文字は和歌を詠むときにしか用いなかった。したがって、

the aristocracy built numerous private temples within the city.

Major temples recruited warrior-monks (*sōhei*) for protection in bitter doctrinal disputes within and among temples and in conflicts over *shōen* holdings. Despite occasional intimidation, the separation of religion and politics was largely maintained. The court nobles remained devout, however, and frequent pilgrimages to major Buddhist and Shintō institutions were common, even for emperors.

The Pure Land doctrine was introduced from China in the ninth century by Ennin and was popularized to some degree by Kūya. The most important Heian figure in Pure Land development was Genshin, who wrote graphically of the horrors of hell and the delights of the Pure Land in the *Ōjōyōshū* (Essentials of Pure Land Rebirth).

Pure Land Buddhism achieved great popularity from mid-Heian times onward. Court nobles and ladies chanted the *nembutsu* with great fervor in the hope of rebirth into the Amida Pure Land or built Amida halls within their residences to show their faith. The most famous example of such private Amida temples is the Phoenix Hall of the Byōdōin.

LITERATURE

The field of literature represented the height of the Heian creative spirit. As in other spheres, a convenient psychological dividing point in Heian literary history is the year 838, when the last official mission was sent to China.

The outburst of literary creativity was made possible by the development of the *kana* syllabary. While it was now theoretically possible to write in Japanese without reliance on any Chinese characters, Heian courtiers remained intellectually committed to the written Chinese language, using *kana* only when composing Japanese poetry. Thus, the use of *kana*

仮名文字を使用したのは大部分が宮廷に仕えた
女房たちで、平安時代の偉大な文学作品を生ん
だのも、ほとんどがこれらの女性たちだった。

廷臣たちは次第に教養として和歌に親しむよ
うになり、事実、和歌の創作は平安時代の宮廷
生活の重要な一面になる。和歌を詠み競う歌合
が開かれ、恋人たちは通常和歌を詠み交わし
た。勅撰和歌集も編纂され、『古今和歌集』はそ
の最高傑作である。

仮名文字は日本固有の散文体の文学を生む
刺激にもなった。平安時代に確立したその基本
形は、物語と日記の2つである。物語文学は
紫式部の『源氏物語』で並ぶもののない高水準
に達している。

日記文学の始まりは、紀貫之が10世紀の初期
に、土佐の国から都への旅を詳細に書き綴った
『土佐日記』であると考えられている。

このジャンルはやがて女性に引き継がれた。
日記文学とは多少系統の異なる文学、清少納言
の『枕草子』は、軽妙な文体で、平安時代の宮
廷人が「おかし」と呼んだ、楽しみあるいは喜び
の理想を示し、随筆という、親しみやすいジャン
ルの先駆けになった。

美術

平安時代の美術は、通常2つの時期に分けられ
る。最初の100年間は、弘仁（810〜824年）ある
いは貞観（859〜877年）という2つの年号にちな
んで、そのどちらかの名称で知られ、後の3世紀
は藤原時代と呼ばれる。貞観時代にはなおも中

was left largely to court ladies, and by and large it was these women who produced the greatest works of Heian literature.

Courtiers turned increasingly to the cultivation of the *waka* poem. In fact, poetry composition became a crucial aspect of the world of the Heian courtier. Poetry competitions were held, and lovers commonly exchanged poems. Imperial anthologies of Japanese poetry were compiled, the *Kokin wakashū* (Collection from Ancient and Modern Times) being perhaps the greatest.

The *kana* syllabary was a stimulus to the creation of a native prose literature, of which there were essentially two types in Heian times: the *monogatari* (tale), and the *nikki* (diary). The former reached unparalleled heights in Murasaki Shikibu's *Genji monogatari* (Tale of Genji).

The *nikki* is regarded as having its beginning with *Tosa nikki* (Tosa Diary), an account by Ki no Tsurayuki of his trip from Tosa Province in the early tenth century. The genre was later taken over by women.

In a slightly different vein from the diary is Sei Shōnagon's *Makura no sōshi* (Pillow Book). The tone is light and witty, expressing the ideal of amusement or delight that Heian courtiers referred to as *okashi*, and this work pioneered the popular genre of essays known as *zuihitsu*.

ART

Heian art is usually divided into two periods. The first 100-year period is known by one of two era names, Kōnin (810–824) or Jōgan (859–877), and the last three centuries are called the Fujiwara age. In the Jōgan era, Chinese influence remained strong, and the development of arts related to eso-

国の影響が強く残り、密教美術の隆盛は人々を
圧倒する。2つの主要な形式は仏像と曼荼羅で
あり、その代表的な例としては、神護寺の薬師
如来像と東寺の両部曼荼羅があげられる。

長期にわたる藤原時代の美術は、文学と同様
に、大きな変化を見せている。阿弥陀如来像が
やがて人気を集め、平等院鳳凰堂の仏師定朝
による阿弥陀如来像はその代表である。

日本的風物を主題にした絵画、大和絵の発達
がこの時代の特色である。風景ならびに宮廷の
日常生活を画題とした屏風絵や襖絵が多く描か
れた。

藤原時代の絵画の優れた例は、11世紀から
12世紀に流行した絵巻物に見られる。有名な歴
史的事件を題材にしたもの、また、仏教の説く
地獄の恐怖や寺院の由来を描いた、宗教色の
濃い作品がある。とりわけ人気が高いのは、紫
式部の偉大な小説の世界を優雅な色彩で描い
た、12世紀の『源氏物語絵巻』だろう。

teric Buddhism was especially striking. The two major art forms were Buddhist sculpture and mandalas. Representative examples include the Yakushi Nyorai at Jingoji and the Ryōbu Mandara at Tōji.

Just as in literature, the art of the long period of Fujiwara domination shows significant development. Images of Amida became popular, the most remarkable being that sculpted by Jōchō in the Phoenix Hall of the Byōdōin.

The most marked departure from earlier art forms was the development of secular painting, known as *yamato-e* or "Japanese (style) pictures." The Fujiwara era witnessed an outburst of secular painting, both landscapes and scenes of daily court life, painted on folding screens (*byōbu*) and on paper doors (*fusuma*).

Perhaps the finest examples of Fujiwara painting are the narrative scrolls (*emakimono*) that came into vogue in the eleventh and twelfth centuries. Some dealt with famous historical incidents while others were more religious in nature, depicting the horrors of Buddhist hell or the origins of a temple. Perhaps the most celebrated is the twelfth-century *Genji monogatari emaki*, which depicts in elegant color the world of Murasaki's great novel.

鎌倉時代
（1185～1333年）

鎌倉時代は鎌倉幕府の存続期間（1192～1333年）とほぼ一致し、その名称は政庁所在地の鎌倉に由来する。鎌倉時代の始まりは、1185年、源頼朝が平氏を滅ぼし、諸国には守護（保安長官、のちに武家領主）、荘園と国衙領（こくがりょう）（地方政府の管理下にある公有地）には地頭（土地・財産管理人）を任命して、武家政権を確立した年である。鎌倉時代の特徴は、地方の武士階級の台頭と武家政権の確立、人々の心をとらえた新仏教の出現と仏教の貴族階級から庶民への普及、それに、文学と美術に漲（みなぎ）る新しい活力である。

背景

1185年、源氏の軍勢は仇敵平氏を壇ノ浦の戦いで打ち破り、ついに源平の争乱に終止符をうった。それに先立って、平氏は保元の乱（1156年）と平治の乱（1160年）の結果、朝廷の支配権を獲得し、源氏を京都から追い払っている。源頼朝が1180年、平氏との戦いを遂行するために設立した小さな司令部、幕府は、1184年には、侍所（さむらいどころ）（軍事・警察）、後に政所（まんどころ）（一般政務）に吸収される公文所（くもんじょ）、それに問注所（もんちゅうじょ）（訴訟・裁判）という3つの役所からなる厖大な組織に成長していた。頼朝はさらに、壇ノ浦の戦いから数か月のうちに、全国に2種類の役人を任命して、配置

Minamoto no Yoritomo
(1147–99). The founder of the Kamakura shogunate, the first warrior government in Japan.

Kamakura Period

(1185–1333)

The Kamakura period corresponds roughly to the span of the Kamakura shogunate (1192–1333) and is named after the city of Kamakura, the seat of government. The period began in 1185, when Minamoto no Yoritomo destroyed the Taira family and established his military government through the appointment of *shugo* (constables; later, military governors) to provinces, and *jitō* (stewards) to *shōen* (landed estates) and *kokugaryō* (lands administered by provincial governments). Distinguishing characteristics of the period are the rise to political power of the provincial warrior class (*bushi*) and the establishment of a military government; the emergence of new and strongly proselytizing sects of Buddhism and the spread of Buddhism from the aristocracy to the common people; and a new vitality in literature and the fine arts.

BACKGROUND

In 1185, Minamoto forces defeated their old rivals, the Taira family, in the Battle of Dannoura, finally bringing to a close the Taira–Minamoto War. Earlier, as a result of the Hōgen Disturbance (1156) and the Heiji Disturbance (1160), the Taira had gained control of the imperial court and had driven the Minamoto out of Kyōto. The small headquarters that Yoritomo had set up in 1180 to prosecute the Taira–Minamoto War had grown by 1184 into a formidable organization of three boards: the Samurai-dokoro, or Board of Retainers; the Kumonjo, or Public Documents Office, which was later absorbed into the Mandokoro, or Administrative Board; and the Monchūjo, or Board of Inquiry. Moreover, within a few

する権限を朝廷から与えられた。守護は法と秩
序を維持するために各国に、地頭は納税義務な
どの遂行を監督するために、荘園と地方政府の
管理下にある公有地に、それぞれ配置されたの
である。そのような広範囲に及ぶ権限が頼朝に
委任されたことは、1192年、彼が朝廷から征夷
大将軍の称号を授けられたことと相まって、京都
の朝廷による鎌倉政権の正式な承認を意味し
た。1192年以降の頼朝の政府は、正式には幕
府と呼ぶべきだろう。それは、日本のその後の
700年間の大部分を支配した一連の武家政権の
始まりである。

武家社会の構造

頼朝の家臣の大部分は高貴な生まれではなか
ったが、頼朝が率いた武家社会は、その考え方
においても、構造においても、明らかに軍事的
な貴族社会だった。この軍事的特権階級の頂点
を占めたのは将軍の家臣、御家人である。御家
人は比較的に少数で、その忠誠心は立証済み
だった。

　御家人の下には侍がいた。侍という言葉は、
後の時代には武士全般を指すようになるが、鎌
倉時代には限られた階級を指していた。御家人
も侍も騎馬武者で、それぞれが自分自身の家臣
を従えていた。

　鎌倉時代の社会が称揚したのは、忠誠心と名
誉と倹約の美徳である。この理想はやがて武士
崇拝の文化、武士道を生む。

months after Dannoura, Yoritomo was given the authority by the imperial court to appoint and post two types of officials throughout the country; a *shugo* to each province to maintain law and order, and *jitō* to private estates and provincial government lands to oversee the fulfillment of obligations, such as the submission of taxes. The delegation of such broad powers to Yoritomo, coupled with the conferral on him in 1192 of the title *seii tai shōgun* ("barbarian-subduing generalissimo") by the imperial court amounted to a formal recognition of the Kamakura government by the imperial government in Kyōto. After 1192, Yoritomo's government may properly be termed a shogunate, and it was to be the first in the succession of such military regimes that ruled Japan for much of the ensuing 700 years.

STRUCTURE OF WARRIOR SOCIETY

Although the majority of Yoritomo's followers were of humble origin, the warrior society that he headed was in outlook and structure a distinct military aristocracy. At the top of this military aristocracy were the shōgun's vassals (*gokenin*). Comparatively few in number, they were men of proven loyalty.

Below them were the *samurai*. In later periods the term came to denote any and all warriors, but in the Kamakura period it referred to a definite rank. Both *gokenin* and samurai were mounted warriors, and each commanded his own following of subvassals.

Kamakura society exalted loyalty, honor, and frugality—ideals that were later to inspire the cult of the warrior, or *bushidō* (literally, "the Way of the Warrior").

北条氏の執権政治

頼朝が揮った権勢は、その一族に長くとどまら
なかった。1199年に頼朝が没すると、2人の若
い息子以外に、その後継者となるめぼしい源氏
の一族はいなかった。頼朝は、平氏を打ち破っ
て、源氏の政権を確立する過程で、弟の源義経
をも含めて、政敵になる恐れのある者をすべて
抹殺していた。鎌倉幕府の実権は頼朝の未亡
人北条政子の一族、北条氏に引き継がれ、鎌倉
時代の終わりまで、彼らが源氏の将軍の執権と
して、全国を統治した。

　全体として、北条氏の統治は安定し有能だっ
た。1221年の承久の乱で、後鳥羽上皇が政権
の奪回を謀ったときにも、2代目の執権北条義時
はその乱を1か月で鎮め、後鳥羽上皇ほか2人
の上皇を配流している。北条義時は最終的に、
将軍の代理人、六波羅探題2人を京都に常駐さ
せて、朝廷の監視に当たらせた。

　北条氏のリーダーのなかで、もっとも資質に恵
まれ、機敏な政治的手腕を示したのは、3代目
の執権北条泰時である。彼は1224年、連署と呼
ばれる役職を新設し、叔父をその職に任じた。
連署は執権と共に公文書に署名し、実際には執
権の補佐役である。

　泰時はまた1225年に、評定衆（国家評議会）を
設置し、幕府への諮問、訴訟の理非の決断、幕
府運営上の重要事項の決定を行う機関としてい
る。5代目の執権北条時頼のもとで、1249年、評
定衆を支援する引付（訴訟機関）も設置される。

　泰時の執政の際立った功績は、1232年の武
士階級の法典、御成敗式目（貞永式目とも呼ば

THE HŌJŌ REGENCY

The power that Yoritomo wielded did not remain in his family for long. When he died in 1199, there were no Minamoto of any importance to succeed him except two young sons, for in the process of defeating the Taira and establishing Minamoto rule he had eliminated all potential rivals, including his younger brother Minamoto no Yoshitsune. Real power passed to the Hōjō family, the family of Yoritomo's widow, Hōjō Masako, and for the remainder of the Kamakura period they ruled the country as regents (*shikken*) to Minamoto shōguns.

On the whole, Hōjō rule was firm and efficient. For example, when the retired emperor Go-Toba attempted to take back the reins of government in the Jōkyū Disturbance of 1221, Hōjō Yoshitoki, the second *shikken*, quelled the uprising within a month and sent Go-Toba and two other former emperors into exile. He then stationed two shogunal deputies (Rokuhara *tandai*) in Kyōto to watch over the court.

The most resourceful and politically astute of the Hōjō leaders was Hōjō Yasutoki, the third *shikken*. In 1224, he created a new office called *rensho*, or cosigner, and appointed his uncle to the post. The *rensho* cosigned with the regent and was, in effect, an associate regent.

In 1225 Yasutoki also established the Hyōjōshū (Council of State), which was the chief advisory, administrative, and judicial body of the Kamakura government. Under Hōjō Tokiyori, the fifth regent, the Hikitsuke (High Court) was created in 1249 to assist the Council of State.

An outstanding accomplishment of Yasutoki's regency was the promulgation in 1232 of a legal code for the warrior

れる)の公布である。御成敗式目は、武士階級
の慣習法と、鎌倉幕府によって確立された判例
などにもとづいて、評定衆によって編纂された、
51か条からなる成文法で、守護や地頭など、幕
府によって任命された役人の義務と責任を明確
にしている。この法典の公布によって、7世紀後
期に確立した律令制度は全面的に廃止され、武
家社会の構造と必要性から生まれた法律がそ
れに取って代わった。

蒙古の襲来

鎌倉時代の最も劇的な事件としてあげられるの
は、8代目の執権北条時宗の時代の蒙古の襲来
である。彼らが最初に襲来したのは1274年、日
本がフビライ・ハン(1215〜94年)の宗主権を認
めることを求めてきたモンゴルの要求をはねつけ
た後である。日本側にとって幸運なことに、約
40,000人の蒙古の軍勢が博多の近くに上陸した
その翌日に、突然の嵐が襲い、蒙古の艦隊の
大半を破壊して、侵略者の多くを溺死させた。

　それから7年後、日本が再びフビライ・ハンの
要求をはねつけ、しかもその使者の首を刎ねる
と、彼は14万から15万人の大軍を博多湾に派遣
した。戦闘が始まって約2か月後に、またしても
激しい台風が起こり、侵略者は退却を強いられ
る。しかし、13世紀の末まで不安を抱き続けた。
幕府は、北条氏の一族を、九州地方の御家人の
間の紛争を解決し、再度の蒙古襲来の際には、
彼らを指揮するという、特別の任務を帯びた幕
府の代理人(鎮西探題)に任命した。

class, the Goseibai Shikimoku (the Formulary of Adjudications; also known as Jōei Shikimoku). Drawn up by the Hyōjōshū and consisting of 51 articles, the code embodied the customary law of the warrior class and judicial precedents established by the Kamakura government. It clarified the duties and responsibilities of Kamakura-appointed officials, such as the *shugo* and the *jitō*. With the promulgation of the Goseibai Shikimoku, the entire *ritsuryō* system, which had been applied since the late seventh century, was swept away and replaced by laws that arose from the structure and requirements of warrior society.

THE MONGOL INVASIONS

Among the most dramatic events of the Kamakura period were the Mongol invasions during the regency of Hōjō Tokimune, the eighth *shikken*. The first was launched in 1274, after the Japanese brusquely rejected a Mongol demand that they acknowledge the sovereignty of Kublai Khan (1215–94). Fortunately for the defenders, only a day after the invading force of about 40,000 men landed near Hakata, a storm suddenly arose, destroying a good part of the fleet and causing many of the invaders to drown.

Seven years later, after the Japanese had rejected his demands once again and, moreover, beheaded his envoys, Kublai dispatched a huge invasion force of between 140,000 and 150,000 men to Hakata Bay. Again, after nearly two months of fighting, a fierce typhoon arose, forcing the invaders to retreat. Until the end of the century the Japanese remained apprehensive. Hōjō family members were appointed special deputies (Chinzei *tandai*) to resolve disputes between shogunal vassals in Kyūshū and to lead them in battle in the event of another attack.

　侵略者の撃退は、国民の自尊心を多少高め、一時的に北条氏の執権政治の面目を施したが、武士たちに約束通りの恩賞を与えることができなかったために、結果的に、国内での紛争を増大させた。海外からの侵略者では、勝利を納めた御家人に与えるための、土地という形態の戦利品が北条氏の手に入らなかったのである。鎌倉幕府は家臣の窮乏を阻止する目的で、法令によって、家臣の保有する土地の売却、あるいはその抵当権の実行を禁止した。この措置は徳政と呼ばれ、その恩恵に浴する者もあったが、債権者の不興を買い、鎌倉幕府にとって、彼らの支持を失うことは大きな痛手になった。

鎌倉時代の経済

鎌倉時代初期に起こり、その全期間にわたって存続した経済的な社会制度は「問丸(といまる)」と「座(ざ)」である。前者は輸送・回漕業者で、米をはじめとする荘園の産物の委託販売を引き受け、広域の市場へ流通させた。後者は同業組合で、しばしば独占主義的な常套手段を用いた。

仏教の大衆化

鎌倉時代の仏教は庶民の信仰を集めた。浄土宗の祖師法然は、個人の努力で悟りに向かうよりも、阿弥陀如来の慈悲にすがれば往生できる、と教えた。法然の弟子親鸞は、浄土真宗の祖師として、行動ではなく、信心こそが救いの基本条件であって、南無阿弥陀仏を専らに唱えれば救われる、と説いた。

　彼らと同程度に論議をかもした宗教活動家日蓮は、日蓮宗を興し、阿弥陀信仰を批判して、

The repulse of the invasions nourished a certain amount of national pride and temporarily raised the prestige of the Hōjō regency; yet the regency could not make good on promises of reward to warriors, and the consequence was increased domestic strife. Because the invaders had come from overseas, the Hōjō could take no war booty in the form of land to grant to its victorious vassals. In an attempt to prevent the increasing impoverishment of its retainers, the shogunate issued decrees forbidding the sale or foreclosure of lands held by its retainers. Called *tokusei*, or "acts of virtuous government," they pleased some but alienated the creditors, whose support the shogunate could ill afford to lose.

THE KAMAKURA-PERIOD ECONOMY

Two economic institutions that arose early in and continued through the Kamakura period were the *toimaru* and the *za*. The former were shipping agents who took rice and other products of the *shōen* on consignment and distributed them over a wide market. The latter were trade guilds that often engaged in monopolistic practices.

POPULARIZATION OF BUDDHISM

During the Kamakura period, Buddhism turned its attention to the common people. Hōnen, founder of the Jōdo sect, taught that reliance on the grace of Amida was more efficacious than personal effort toward enlightenment. His disciple Shinran, founder of the Jōdo Shin sect, held that faith, not acts, was the one essential qualification for salvation, which could be achieved by a single invocation of Amida's name.

An equally controversial religious figure was Nichiren, founder of the Nichiren sect, who criticized the Amida sects

仏教の基本的な教えは法華経にある、と主張している。

　鎌倉時代に栄えたもう1つの仏教は禅宗である。その単純さと、悟りを開くために、自戒と坐禅を強調する点は、とりわけ武士階級の感性に訴えた。臨済宗を伝えた栄西と、曹洞宗を伝えた道元は、彼らにその教義、儀式、さらに宗派の名称までも授けた中国の禅僧たちの弟子を自任している。

文学と美術

朝廷は政治的な役割を奪われたとはいえ、なおも日本の文化の中心だった。第8番目の勅撰和歌集『新古今和歌集』が編纂されたのは1205年である。鴨長明（かものちょうめい）は、政権が朝廷から地方へ移行する過程で起こった惨劇を目撃し、人間の営みの無常を『方丈記』（ほうじょうき）に書き綴った。

　とはいえ、鎌倉時代を代表する散文体の文学形式は軍記物語で、その最も有名なものは『平家物語』である。琵琶の伴奏に合わせて吟じられるこの物語は、仏教的な無常観を背景に、平家の興亡を語る。1275年、北条実時は、和漢書の図書館、金沢文庫を設立した。

　鎌倉時代の優れた美術品としては、運慶と快慶の木彫が特筆に値する。東大寺南大門の巨大な仁王像は、2人の共作による。鎌倉時代の絵師は肖像画に強い関心と技術を示し、とりわけ有名な例としては、藤原隆信の作と伝えられる源頼朝像があげられる。

One of Benevolent King (Niō) statues, produced at the workshop of Unkei and Kaikei, stand guard at the south gate of the temple Tōdaiji in Nara.

and insisted that the essential teachings of Buddhism were contained in the Lotus Sutra.

Another form of Buddhism that flourished in this period was Zen. Its simplicity and emphasis on self-discipline and meditation as the means to enlightenment particularly appealed to the warrior class. Both Eisai, who introduced the Rinzai sect, and Dōgen, who introduced the Sōtō sect, considered themselves disciples of Chinese Zen masters from whom they received teachings, ritual, and even the names of their sects.

LITERATURE AND THE FINE ARTS

Although deprived of its political role, the court remained the center of Japanese culture. The *Shin kokin wakashū* (New Collection from Ancient and Modern Times), the eighth imperial anthology, appeared in 1205. Kamo no Chōmei had witnessed the terrible events that accompanied the transfer of power from the court to the provinces, and in the *Hōjōki* (The Ten Foot Square Hut), he dwells upon the impermanence of all human endeavor (*mujō*).

The characteristic form of Kamakura-period prose literature, however, was the *gunki monogatari*, or war tale. The most famous of these was *Heike monogatari* (The Tale of the Heike). Recited to the accompaniment of the *biwa*, the story recounts the rise and fall of the Taira in the context of the Buddhist philosophy of impermanence. In 1275, Hōjō Sanetoki established Kanazawa Bunko, a library of Chinese and Japanese manuscripts.

Among accomplishments in the fine arts during the Kamakura period, the wood sculptures of Unkei and Kaikei, who collaborated on the two huge guardian deities of the great south gate (*nandaimon*) at Tōdaiji, are of particular note. Painters of the era showed a great interest and skill in portraiture, a particularly renowned example of which is the portrait of Minamoto no Yoritomo attributed to Fujiwara no Takanobu.

幕府の衰退と崩壊

鎌倉幕府は1333年、2人の重要な武将の裏切り
で、突然の終わりを迎えた。足利尊氏は隠岐か
ら脱出した後醍醐天皇の懲罰のために派遣さ
れるが、彼はその遠征の途中で後醍醐天皇の
支持にまわる(建武の中興)。もう1人の武将新田
義貞は尊氏を攻めるよう命じられるが、彼もまた、
反旗を翻し、14代執権北条高時に自刃を強い
る。こうして150年に及ぶ日本で最初の軍事政
権の時代は終わる。

DECLINE AND FALL OF THE SHOGUNATE

The Kamakura shogunate came to a sudden end in 1333 when two important vassals turned against their leader. Ashikaga Takauji had been sent on a punitive expedition against the retired emperor Go-Daigo, who had recently escaped from the island of Oki, but Takauji chose instead to support Go-Daigo (Kemmu Restoration). Another vassal of the shogunate, Nitta Yoshisada, was ordered to proceed against Takauji, but he too turned against his superiors and forced Hōjō Takatoki, the fourteenth regent, to take his own life. Thus ended the 150-year rule of the country's first military regime.

室町時代

(1333〜1568年)

足利尊氏の率いる軍勢が鎌倉幕府を滅ぼした1333年から、覇者織田信長が京都を占領した1568年まで続く、文化的発展と社会的混乱の時代。その名称は幕府の本営、将軍の御所のあった京都の室町に由来し、室町時代は1338年から1573年まで将軍の座を占めた一族に因んで、足利時代とも呼ばれる。

　1337年から1392年の期間は、2つの朝廷が対立して存在し、それぞれが皇統の正当性を主張した。この時代は南北朝時代と呼ばれている。

　応仁の乱(1467〜77年)が始まった年から、織田信長が入京した1568年までの期間は、ときには戦国時代とも呼ばれ、この時代を特徴づけるのは、下剋上(げこくじょう)(下の者が上の者を凌いで倒す)という言葉である。

政治の展開：中央政府

足利尊氏は鎌倉幕府の人材と機構を借りて、室町幕府を設立した。足利尊氏をはじめ、彼を補佐して建武式目(けんむしきもく)と呼ばれる施政の基本方針を起草した武士たちは、北条家のもと御家人だった。

　とはいえ、その体制は鎌倉幕府と異なり、守護に任命した御家人に対する足利氏の支配力は、最初から弱かった。斯波氏、細川氏、畠山氏など、有力な守護の一族は、将軍補佐(管領)

Muromachi Period

(1333–1568)

A period of cultural achievement and social disorder, lasting from 1333, when forces led by Ashikaga Takauji destroyed the Kamakura shogunate, until 1568, when hegemon Oda Nobunaga captured the capital of Kyōto. Named for the district of Kyōto in which the shogunal residence was situated, it is also commonly known as the Ashikaga period, after the family that held the position of shōgun from 1338 to 1573.

Between 1337 and 1392, the two rival courts co-existed, each claiming the legitimate right to rule. This period is known as the Nambokuchō period (the period of the Northern and Southern Courts).

The years from the beginning of Ōnin War (1467–77) until Oda Nobunaga entered Kyōto in 1568 are sometimes referred to as the Sengoku period (Warring States period). The term *gekokujō* (the overturning of those on top by those below) characterizes this period.

POLITICAL DEVELOPMENTS: CENTRAL GOVERNMENT

In establishing the Muromachi shogunate, Ashikaga Takauji borrowed personnel and institutions from the Kamakura shogunate. He and the warriors who helped him draft the statement of legal and political principles known as the Kemmu Shikimoku (Kemmu Code) of 1336 had been vassals of the Hōjō family.

However, unlike the Kamakura regime, Ashikaga control over the vassals they appointed as *shugo* was weak from the outset. Powerful *shugo* families such as the Shiba family, the Hosokawa family, and the Hatakeyama family were able to

の重職を独占して、幕政の中枢を支配した。初
期の足利将軍数人は、その権威を示すことがで
きたが、後の将軍たちには、守護の連合体の指
揮をとる力はなかった。

室町幕府は出発点から困難を抱えていた。足
利尊氏は弟の足利直義に行政と司法の責任の
大半を任せ、彼自身は侍所と恩賞方を支配し
た。この権限の分担は、やがて兄弟の反目に発
展し、南朝方の追討と地方で強大化する守護の
制圧を阻む。後醍醐天皇の死と直義の暗殺に
よって、尊氏の地位は多少強化されるが、尊氏
が死んだ1358年には、足利氏の支配権はまだ
安定したとは言えなかった。

Ashikaga Yoshimitsu
(1358–1408). Third
shōgun of the
Muromachi shogunate
and builder of the
temple Kinkakuji in
Kyōto.

足利尊氏の後継者、足利義詮と足利義満は
全国的に将軍の支配力を強めることができた。
義満は1369年、11歳で将軍に任命され、管領細
川頼之の補佐のもと禅僧義堂周信の宗教面な
らびに文化面の指導を受けて、精力的で、教養
のある統治者に成長した。義満は1395年、太政
大臣という最高位の官職を与えられている。義
満は西日本の守護に命じて1390年の土岐氏の
乱、1391年の山名氏の乱（明徳の乱）、1399〜
1400年の大内氏の乱（応永の乱）を鎮圧した。
全国で彼の全面的な支配が及ばなかった重要
な地域は東日本だけであった。

義満は、能楽の観阿弥や世阿弥、朝廷歌人
の二条良基、禅僧の絶海中津など、趣味や文芸

monopolize the important office of shogunal deputy (*kanrei*) and to dominate the senior councils of the shogunate. Several of the earlier Ashikaga rulers were able to impose their authority, but later shōguns were much less successful in managing the coalition of *shugo*.

The Muromachi shogunate got off to a troubled start. Takauji allowed considerable administrative and judicial responsibility to his younger brother, Ashikaga Tadayoshi, while reserving for himself authority over the Samurai-dokoro (Board of Retainers) and Onshō-gata (Office of Rewards). The division of authority decayed into a breach between the brothers that hampered both the conduct of campaigns against the Southern Court loyalists and containment of the local aggrandizements of *shugo*. The death of Emperor Go-Daigo and the assassination of Tadayoshi left Takauji in a stronger position, yet Ashikaga control was far from secure at his death in 1358.

His successors Ashikaga Yoshiakira and Ashikaga Yoshimitsu were able to increase shogunal authority over the country. Appointed shōgun in 1369 at the age of 11, Yoshimitsu, under the secular tutelage of shogunal deputy Hosokawa Yoriyuki and the religious and cultural guidance of the Zen monk Gidō Shūshin, grew into a vigorous, cultivated ruler. In 1395, Yoshimitsu was granted the highest court office, *dajō daijin* (grand minister of state). He took the lead in organizing vassals in western Japan to crush uprisings by the Toki family in 1390, the Yamana family in 1391 (Meitoku Rebellion), and the Ōuchi family in 1399–1400 (Ōei Rebellion). The only important area of the country that remained outside the full scope of his control was eastern Japan.

Yoshimitsu surrounded himself with such arbiters of taste and literary style as the Nō dramatists Kan'ami and

の権威を取り立て、能楽、和歌、絵画、造園を
支援した。彼の「花の御所」と「北山第」(後の金
閣寺)は、やがて文化と知的教養の重要な中心
になる。

　1401年、義満は中国の明朝と勘合貿易を開
始した。10年間に8回の使節団がその航海を完
了している。

　室町幕府の権威は義満の息子、足利義持の
代に衰退した。義持は1417年の上杉禅秀の乱
の鎮圧に成功するが、彼の政治にかける情熱は
一貫性を欠いていた。幕府の権威は独裁的な
6代将軍足利義教によって一時的に回復される。
彼は義持が中断した勘合貿易を再開し、また、
管領と守護の影響力の排除を図っている。義教
の政策は一時的に将軍の支配力を強めるが、彼
のとった横暴な手段は朝廷と守護の反感を買
い、1441年の守護赤松満祐による義教の暗殺
は、足利政権の崩壊の始まりになった。

　8代将軍足利義政の時代には、幕府の全国的
な統治力はほとんどなかった。義政は債務に苦
しむ武士や農民の要求に応じ、「徳政令」によっ
て、金融業者、商人、寺院などの債権を無効に
した。この債務の弁済の一時的な延期(徳政)
は、市場を混乱に陥れ、さらに、それを廃止し
ようとする義政の優柔不断な試みは、暴動や略
奪を引き起こした。義政の別邸、銀閣の造営は、
すでに逼迫していた幕府の資金を枯渇させ、彼
が正室日野富子の要請で後継者を変えたこと
は、細川氏と山名氏をそれぞれのリーダーとし
て敵対する守護を巻き込む紛争を引き起こし、

Zeami, the courtier-poet Nijō Yoshimoto, and the Zen master Zekkai Chūshin, and patronized Nō, poetry, painting, and garden design. His "Palace of Flowers" (Hana no Gosho) and his Kitayama villa (later converted into Kinkakuji) became vital cultural and intellectual centers.

In 1401, Yoshimitsu initiated the tally trade (*kangō bōeki*) with Ming dynasty China. During a period of ten years, eight embassies completed the sea voyage.

The power and prestige of the shogunate declined under Yoshimitsu's son Ashikaga Yoshimochi. Although he succeeded in putting down the Rebellion of Uesugi Zenshū in 1417, his commitment to government was erratic. Shogunal authority was reasserted briefly by the despotic sixth shōgun, Ashikaga Yoshinori. He reopened the China trade, which Yoshimochi had broken off, and worked to offset the influence of the *kanrei* and *shugo*. Yoshinori's policies briefly strengthened the shogunate, but his brutal methods antagonized courtiers and *shugo*, and his assassination in 1441 by Akamatsu Mitsusuke, one of his own vassals, marked the beginning of the disintegration of Ashikaga authority.

Under the eighth shōgun, Ashikaga Yoshimasa, shogunal influence over the country all but collapsed. Responding to demands by indebted warriors and peasants, Yoshimasa issued "acts of virtuous government" (*tokusei*), canceling debts owed moneylenders, merchants, and temples. These debt moratoriums threw the markets into confusion and Yoshimasa's vacillating attempts to revoke them provoked riots and pillaging. His construction of an elegant villa, the Ginkakuji (Silver Pavilion), depleted already straitened shogunal coffers, and his change of mind over a successor at the insistence of his consort Hino Tomiko created a dispute that drew into its vortex rival leagues of *shugo* led by the

これが応仁の乱の始まりになった。両軍の抗争
によって京都は灰燼に帰し、将軍は管領の地位
を独占した細川氏によって、意のままに更迭さ
れた。

政治的展開：地方政府

足利氏のもとで、朝廷による地方の統治機構は
完全に消滅した。地方の行政と司法の責任は守
護に割り当てられた。守護はその権限を目一杯
に利用して強大化し、地方の軍事的な支配者に
なった。歴史家は彼らを守護大名と呼んでいる。

　足利義満による幕府の支配権の統合によっ
て、守護は多かれ少なかれ、京都に定住するこ
とを余儀なくされた。彼らの領国は守護代に任
され、守護代と国人（地方に住みついている武
士）との権力闘争によって苦しめられた。農民の
暴動は増加し、年貢が守護の手元に届かない
ことも多かった（国一揆）。守護大名の大半は15
世紀の末に没落し、彼らの領国は戦国大名の
支配下で、より小さな単位に分割された。

　戦国大名はその領国に住み、彼ら自身の軍
事力、政治力、経済力の強化に精力を注いだ。
彼らは分国法を定め、城下町を築き、検地を行
い、荘園を解体し、土一揆を鎮圧して、農村を
厳しい監督のもとに置いたのである。

経済と社会

室町時代には経済活動が飛躍的に発達し、力
をつけた商人グループと、ますます反抗的にな

Hosokawa and Yamana, thus commencing the Ōnin War. The contesting armies reduced Kyōto to ashes. Shōguns were appointed and deposed almost at will by the Hosokawa family, which monopolized the post of *kanrei*.

POLITICAL DEVELOPMENTS: LOCAL GOVERNMENT

Under the Ashikaga the imperial institutions of local control withered completely. Provinces were assigned to the administrative and judicial authority of *shugo*. Making full use of their powers, *shugo* succeeded in aggrandizing themselves and became provincial military lords. They are referred to by historians as *shugo daimyō*.

With the consolidation of shogunal authority by Yoshimitsu, the *shugo* were obliged to reside more or less permanently in Kyōto. Entrusted to deputies (*shugodai*), their provinces were racked by power struggles between the *shugodai* and *kokujin* (resident local warriors); peasant uprisings increased and tax income often failed to reach the *shugo* (*kuni ikki*). The majority of *shugo* houses were toppled in the late fifteenth century and their regional domains were carved up into more compact units under the control of warlords (Sengoku daimyō).

The Sengoku daimyō lived in their domains, devoting their energies to improving their own military, political, and economic strength. Their activities encompassed promulgating law codes (*bunkokuhō*), building castle towns, conducting land surveys (*kenchi*), breaking up *shōen*, crushing peasant uprisings, and bringing villages under close supervision.

ECONOMY AND SOCIETY

The Muromachi period witnessed a quantum leap forward in economic activity and the emergence of two powerful social

り、市場経済に適応した農民階級という、2つの強力な社会勢力が現れる。

　農業生産の増大、手工業の発達、米や布に代わって現金で求められた租税の納入などは、地方の市場の拡大と、商業の専門化、それに、より高度な取引施設の発達を促した。室町時代には、中国から輸入された銅銭（永楽銭）がさらに大量に流通するようになり、貨幣経済はめざましい発達を遂げる。

　市は月に6日、定期的に開かれた。商工業者は自ら「座」と呼ばれる、西欧のギルドに似た同業組合を結成した。「座」は増大する商業活動に秩序を与えたが、同時に地方の商工業者の参入を阻むことを目的としたため、16世紀の半ば以降、戦国大名は多くの法令によって市場を解放した（楽市と楽座）。

　かつて険しい山の上に築かれていた城は、戦国大名によって平地に築かれ、速やかに市街地の中心になった。港、市の立つ土地、それに交通の要衝に、新しい都市が続々と生まれた。堺、博多、それに兵庫は海外貿易で栄えた。坂本は延暦寺の門前町として発展し、宇治山田は伊勢神宮の参拝者で賑わった。

　戦国大名はその城下町に独裁的な支配権を揮った。しかし、それ以外の都市では、自治的な政治も行われた。堺では、36人の有力な市民が組織した「会合衆」と呼ばれる評議会が、市政を運営した。京都では、各地区の住民グループ（町衆）が地区（町）の自治・自衛の責任を負った。

forces, a self-conscious mercantile group and an increasingly restive and market-oriented peasantry.

Increases in agricultural output, the growth of crafts, and demands for payment of taxes and levies in cash instead of in rice or cloth contributed to the spread of local markets, to greater specialization among merchants, and to more sophisticated exchange facilities. Increasing quantities of copper cash (*eirakusen*) were imported from China during the period and monetization of the economy expanded.

Markets (*ichi*) were held regularly on six days of the month. Merchants and craftsmen organized themselves in guild-like associations known as *za*. *Za* served to bring order to the growing commercial activity. However, they also sought to block participation by provincial merchants and craftsmen, and from the mid-sixteenth century, Sengoku daimyō issued a spate of edicts freeing markets (*rakuichi* and *rakuza*; free markets and open guilds).

Castles, which had formerly been built on craggy peaks, were erected on the plains by Sengoku daimyō and quickly grew into urban centers. New towns sprang up at ports, market sites, and transportation nodes. Sakai, Hakata, and Hyōgo grew rich on the overseas trade. Sakamoto developed as the supply point for the temple Enryakuji, and Uji-Yamada benefited from the influx of pilgrims to Ise Shrine.

Daimyō exercised autocratic control over their castle towns. In other towns, however, self-governing civic communities emerged. Thirty-six leading citizens in Sakai formed a council known as the *egōshū* (city elders), which governed the city. In Kyōto groups of townsmen (*machishū*) were responsible for governance of the districts (*machi*).

宗教と文化

禅宗は足利将軍の保護のもとで急速に発展した。臨済宗の五山組織は全国に広がり、地方武士の子弟に座禅と学芸を教えている。一山一寧などの中国の禅僧は、禅の実践方法と仏教の経典ばかりでなく、朱子学と中国の詩や絵画を日本に伝えた。中国の水墨画は雪舟等楊によって広められ、禅宗寺院の外部にも普及する。狩野派初期の絵師、狩野正信と狩野元信は、中国の水墨画に大和絵の伝統を取り入れた。

室町時代には、他の宗派の仏教の影響も広範囲に及んだ。日蓮宗は関東地方の武士の信仰を集めた。浄土真宗の熱狂的な信者は、15世紀に本願寺の指導下で、蓮如によって組織され、大規模な暴動（一向一揆）を起こして戦国大名に対抗した。キリスト教もまた、1549年のフランシスコ・ザビエルの来日によって、日本に伝えられている。

室町文化は、貴族的要素と、庶民の要素の微妙な混合である。天皇や廷臣たちが武士の上層部と、能楽や狂言、また、歴史物語『増鏡』や軍記物語『太平記』に対する興味を分かち合い、さらに、そのいずれもが御伽草子と呼ばれる庶民的な短編物語や田楽、連歌などの楽しみを庶民と分かち合ったのである。

Francis Xavier (1506–52). He introduced Christianity to Japan and set up the first Christian mission in the country.

RELIGION AND CULTURE

Zen Buddhism developed rapidly under the patronage of the Ashikaga shōguns. The Gozan network of the Rinzai sect covered Japan and gave training in meditation and the arts to the sons of provincial warriors. Chinese priests, such as Issan Ichinei, introduced to Japan not only Zen practices and Buddhist texts but also Neo-Confucian political thought (Shushigaku) and Chinese poetry and painting. Chinese ink-painting was carried outside Zen cloisters by Sesshū Tōyō. Under the early Kanō school masters Kanō Masanobu and Kanō Motonobu, the Chinese style of ink-painting was blended with the techniques of Japanese-style painting.

The influence of other sects of Buddhism also spread widely during the Muromachi period. The Nichiren sect attracted many samurai followers in the Kantō region. Adherents of the Jōdo Shin sect, organized under the leadership of the temple Honganji by Rennyo in the fifteenth century, mounted large-scale uprisings (Ikkō *ikki*) against the Sengoku daimyō. With the arrival of Francis Xavier in 1549, Christianity was also introduced to Japan.

Muromachi culture was an intricate blending of elite and popular elements. Emperors and courtiers shared with high-ranking warriors an interest in Nō and *kyōgen* as well as in the historical chronicles and war tales of the age like *Masukagami* and *Taiheiki* (Chronicle of the Great Peace), and both shared with commoners a passion for the short tales known as *otogi-zōshi* (companion stories), dance and mime (*dengaku*), and linked verse (*renga*).

安土桃山時代

（1568〜1600年）

安土桃山時代という短い、しかし劇的な時
代に、日本の社会と文化は中世から近世
へと移行した。ヨーロッパの商人とカトリックの宣
教師の日本における活動は、日本人の海外進
出に劣らず、この時代を国際色豊かなものにし
ている。

　安土桃山時代に、日本は1世紀に及ぶ内乱を
終結させて統一を果たした。日本の再統一をも
たらしたのは、3人の覇者、織田信長、豊臣秀
吉、それに徳川家康である。

　この時代の名称は、2つの城の所在地、すな
わち信長の壮麗な居城のあった安土と、秀吉の
本営のあった伏見の桃山に由来する。

Oda Nobunaga
(1534–82). The prime
mover of Japan's
16th-century
reunification after a
hundred years of strife.

安土桃山時代の支配体制の発展

安土桃山時代に発達した中央集権制度は織豊
体制と呼ばれる。織田信長と豊臣秀吉は日本
の軍事的な再統一を果たしたばかりではなく、
社会を全国的な規模で支配する新しい方法を
考え出した。

　1568年の信長の入京は、この体制の始まりに
なった。彼が建て前として掲げた目標は、「正
統」の候補者、足利義昭を室町幕府の将軍の座
に据えることだった。信長は政治の中枢で指導
者的な役割を演じることによって、自らの権威と
支配力を強めようとした。

　将軍義昭はまもなく信長を倒そうとする諸大名
や寺院と手を結んだ。信長は京都の大半を焼

Azuchi-Momoyama Period

(1568–1600)

During the Azuchi-Momoyama period, a short but spectacular epoch, Japanese society and culture underwent the transition from the medieval to the early modern era. The activities of European traders and Catholic missionaries in Japan, no less than Japanese ventures overseas, gave the period a cosmopolitan flavor.

Azuchi-Momoyama witnessed Japan's unification after a century of civil war. The country was reunited by three hegemons, Oda Nobunaga, Toyotomi Hideyoshi, and Tokugawa Ieyasu.

The period is named after the sites of two castles, Nobunaga's palatial fortress at Azuchi and Hideyoshi's headquarters at Momoyama in Fushimi.

INSTITUTIONAL DEVELOPMENTS OF THE PERIOD

The central governmental system that developed in Japan during the Azuchi-Momoyama period is called the Shokuhō regime. Oda Nobunaga and Toyotomi Hideyoshi not only reunified Japan militarily; they devised new measures to regulate society on a nationwide basis.

Nobunaga's march on Kyōto in 1568 initiated the regime. His ostensible purpose was to install the "legitimate" claimant, Ashikaga Yoshiaki, in the Muromachi shogunate. Nobunaga wanted to enhance his own prestige and power by playing the lead role on the central stage of politics.

Yoshiaki soon banded with secular and religious lords intent on destroying Nobunaga. The hegemon responded by

き払って対抗したが、将軍は屈しなかった。
1573年8月、信長は義昭を京都から追放するが、
義昭は1588年まで退位を拒否する。したがって
形式的には室町幕府もそれまで存続する。

信長は同じ1573年に、朝倉義景と浅井長政
を滅ぼす。1575年の決定的な対決、長篠の戦
いでは、信長の近代的な鉄砲隊戦術が、武田
勝頼の中世の騎馬武者を戦場から一掃した。
1575年には、信長はさらに、越前の武装した本
願寺門徒集団（一向一揆）を制圧し、1580年に
は、石山本願寺を落とし、門徒の支配下にあっ
た加賀を取り上げた。1582年、信長は武田勝頼
を滅ぼし、配下の武将に、武田家の所領を配分
した。

1582年、信長が本能寺の変で倒れたとき、彼
の支配下にあった領域、いわゆる「天下」は日本
の68か国のうち30か国に及んだ。日本の中央
部は単一政権のもとに再統一されていたのである。
とはいえ、全国的には、広範な地域がなおも服従
を拒み、全国統一達成への道はまだ遠かった。

その任務を完遂したのは信長のかつての部
下、豊臣秀吉である。彼は先ず、信長の暗殺者
明智光秀を山崎の戦いで滅ぼした。本能寺の
変のわずか11日後である。その翌年、秀吉は越
前と加賀の支配者柴田勝家を賤ヶ岳の戦いで
打ち破った。そして1583年には、本州の最西部
に広大な領地を持つ大名毛利輝元との和解に
達している。1585年の初めには、徳川家康もま
た、前年の小牧長久手の戦いで秀吉と争い、引
き分けでそれを終結させたあと、秀吉に従うこ

Toyotomi Hideyoshi
(1537–98). The warlord
Hideyoshi is said to
have been small in
stature, wearing
oversized clothes and a
false mustache in
order to look more
impressive.

burning the greater part of Kyōto but the shōgun remained belligerent. In August 1573 Nobunaga drove Yoshiaki from Kyōto. Yoshiaki would refuse to abdicate until 1588, and the Muromachi shogunate therefore retained a shadowy legal identity.

In that same year of 1573, Nobunaga crushed Asakura Yoshikage and Asai Nagamasa. At the crucial battle of Nagashino in 1575, his modern musketry tactics swept the medieval chivalry of Takeda Katsuyori from the battlefield. Also in 1575, Nobunaga conquered Echizen Province from the armed adherents (Ikkō *ikki*) of the Honganji. In 1580, the Honganji itself surrendered and its provincial domain in Kaga was conquered. In 1582, Nobunaga destroyed Katsuyori and distributed the Takeda domains among his own victorious generals.

When Nobunaga was killed in the Honnōji Incident of 1582, the "realm" (*tenka*) governed by his regime covered no less than thirty of Japan's sixty-eight provinces. Central Japan had been reunited under one political authority. Great areas of the country, however, remained unsubdued. The task of national unification was far from over.

That task was completed by Nobunaga's erstwhile subordinate, Toyotomi Hideyoshi. First he destroyed Nobunaga's assassin, Akechi Mitsuhide, at the Battle of Yamazaki, a mere eleven days after the Honnōji Incident. The next year, Hideyoshi defeated Shibata Katsuie, the ruler of Echizen and Kaga, at the Battle of Shizugatake. By 1583, Hideyoshi had reached an accommodation with Mōri Terumoto, the lord of vast territories in westernmost Honshū. Early in 1585, Toku-gawa Ieyasu too agreed to subordinate himself to Hideyoshi, after fighting him to a standoff in the Komaki Nagakute

とに同意した。1585年、秀吉は四国を平定し、1587年には九州を攻略して、島津氏を降伏させた。それから3年後、秀吉は傘下の大名の軍勢を率いて、小田原の北条氏を攻め、関東地方を平定している（小田原征伐）。

　北部の陸奥と出羽では、領主の対立が続いていたが、秀吉は腹心の武将の率いる軍勢を派遣して、この広大な地域を平定した。1591年の10月末には、抵抗の痕跡さえも拭い去られている。秀吉は初めてその支配体制を全国に広げたといえる。

　地域の領主たちは秀吉の全国的な支配体制に組み込まれた。秀吉が彼らの存在を認める限りは、彼らはその家来と領民を全面的に支配する大名になれた。彼らが支払った代償は、自らの独立を秀吉に引き渡すことだった。武士は農村から城下町に移され、官僚的な支配階級になる運命を担ったのである。

　秀吉は1588年の全国的な刀狩令によって、農民から武器を取り上げた。そして1591年には、武士、農民、それに商人の身分の変更を禁止した。

　1598年、秀吉が没したときには、彼の命じた土地台帳測量（検地）は全国に広がっていた。耕作可能な土地は全て、この検地によって測量され、評価された。そのうえで農産物の推定生産高が、村ごとに用意された土地台帳（検地帳）に記入された。このような土地台帳への登録は、村人たちの土地保有権をこれまでになく確実に保証し、増産を促している。

　織田・豊臣の支配体制は従来の中世的な政治秩序に取って代わったが、その体制を正当化

Campaign the previous year. In 1585, Hideyoshi conquered Shikoku; in 1587, he overran Kyūshū, bringing the Shimazu to heel. Three years later, he led the armies of his vassal daimyō against the Hōjō of Odawara and subjugated the Kantō region (Odawara Campaign).

The northern provinces of Mutsu and Dewa remained an arena of internecine struggle. Hideyoshi sent armies under his principal generals to sweep this giant region; by the end of October 1591 they had wiped out all traces of resistance. Hideyoshi could for the first time truly claim that he had extended his regime nationwide.

The provincial lords were integrated into Hideyoshi's national regime. Insofar as Hideyoshi recognized their autonomous existence, they were transformed into daimyō with full authority over their vassals and the populace of their domains. The price they paid was the surrender of their independence to him. Removed from the countryside to the castle town, the military men were destined to turn into a class of bureaucratic administrators.

Hideyoshi's national sword-hunt decree of 1588 disarmed the countrymen. In 1591, Hideyoshi prohibited the change of status among samurai, farmer, and merchant.

By the time of Hideyoshi's death in 1598, the great wave of cadastral surveys (*kenchi*) ordained by him had covered the entire country. All the arable land was measured and assessed by these surveys; its putative agricultural yield was entered on cadastral registers (*kenchichō*) prepared village by village. Being listed in these registers gave the villagers an unprecedented security of tenure, which served as an incentive to increase production.

The Oda-Toyotomi regime displaced the long-established medieval political order, but it lacked its own, clearly formu-

するための、明確に構築された政治理論を欠いていた。信長には、彼自身の政治的な創造物天下のためのイデオロギーを開発する時間がなかった。秀吉は伝統的な権威の象徴を利用して、自らの正当性を取り付けた。その顕著な例は高貴な官職で、天皇から1585年に授与された関白、さらに1587年1月に授与された太政大臣である。

　秀吉の死後、野心的な家来の抗争によってその支配体制は分裂した。そのなかで最も力があったのは徳川家康である。

安土桃山時代の文化

この時代の最大の象徴は城である。城は権力の象徴として壮大な規模で築かれ、贅沢な装飾を施されて、見る人を威圧することを目的としていた。城にほぼ匹敵する象徴は茶室である。茶室は四畳半で、装飾を控え、そこに坐れば外界から離れて、独りになれるように設計された、美意識を呼び覚ます空間である。

　侘茶(簡素静寂の境地を重んじる茶の湯)の理想を体現する人物、としばしば言われる豪商千利休は、教養を身につけることに熱心だった権力者秀吉に、茶の湯の師匠として仕えた。

　安土桃山時代に製作依頼の多かった美術品は、大規模な障壁画と屏風絵である。最も有名な絵師は、信長の安土城や秀吉の京都の聚楽第など、壮麗な居城の装飾を担った狩野永徳である。

　狩野永徳と同時代の絵師、水墨画の海北友松と長谷川等伯は、時代の好みに速やかに順応して、金碧障壁画の傑作を生んだ。

lated justification in political theory. Nobunaga had not been granted the time to develop an ideology for his own political creation, the *tenka*. Hideyoshi drew his legitimation from the use of the traditional symbols of authority associated with it. These included most prominently the lofty aristocratic offices of *kampaku* (imperial regent), which he had the emperor invest him with in 1585, and of *dajō daijin* (grand minister of state), which he obtained in January 1587.

Upon Hideyoshi's death, the regime was rent by the competing ambitions of his vassals, among whom Tokugawa Ieyasu proved to be the most powerful.

THE CULTURE OF THE PERIOD

The greatest symbol of Azuchi-Momoyama is the castle—a representation of power, built on a grand scale, decorated lavishly, and meant to overawe the viewer. A nearly coequal symbol is the teahouse—an evocation of aestheticism, content with a space nine feet square, eschewing ornamental decor, and designed to permit the visitor to withdraw into solitude from the world of affairs.

Sen no Rikyū, a rich merchant often described as the very incarnation of the ideals of *wabicha* (a type of tea ceremony supposedly governed by restraint), served as tea master to that powerful aspirant to cultural accomplishment, Hideyoshi.

The period's most important artistic commissions were large-scale wall paintings and paintings on folding screens (*byōbu*). The most renowned master was Kanō Eitoku, who decorated several palatial residences, including Nobunaga's Azuchi Castle and Hideyoshi's Jurakudai in Kyōto.

Eitoku's other great contemporaries, Kaihō Yūshō and Hasegawa Tōhaku, who were specialists in ink painting, adapted themselves more readily to the tastes of the times

　　イエズス会の宣教師はヨーロッパから大量の
宗教画を輸入した。日本人絵師はこれらの絵を
手本にして、ヨーロッパ人を基本テーマにした洋
風の作品（南蛮美術）を生み出している。

　　安土桃山時代の文学には、美術に見られるほ
どの華麗さはない。文学的な活力は衰え、新し
い分野はまだ芽生えたばかりだった。この時代
に現れた興味深い事業としては、イエズス会宣
教団の切支丹版がある。宗教的な作品が主で
あったが、『イソップ物語』の日本語訳など多様
な文学作品も出版されている。

安土桃山時代の国際的な側面
この時代の際立った国際色のほとんどは、新た
に加わったヨーロッパの商人とカトリックの宣教
師の存在によってもたらされた。日本はヨーロッ
パの文明に、初めて直接触れたのである。この
国際的な時代は1563年、九州の大名大村純忠
がポルトガルとの貿易をすすめるために、彼ら
の支持するイエズス会の宣教師から洗礼を受
け、最初のキリシタン大名になった年から、1597
年、26人の日本の殉教者が秀吉の命令によって
磔刑に処され（26聖人殉教）、キリスト教徒の血
なまぐさい迫害が始まった年まで続く。
　　1582年、キリシタンの日本人少年4人が、九州
のキリシタン大名の使節として、教皇グレゴリオ
13世に謁見するために、ローマに派遣された（天
正遣欧使節）。しかし派遣中にキリスト教の禁令
が出たために、彼らは1590年に帰国後、その経
験を公表することができなかった。

and produced masterpieces in rich, gilded polychrome.

The Jesuits imported from Europe a large number of religious paintings. These paintings served as models for Japanese artists. They produced works in Western styles taking Europeans as their principal theme (*namban* art; "Southern barbarian" art).

In the history of literature, Azuchi-Momoyama cannot boast a similar richness. The vital force of the literati was expiring, while new traditions were barely beginning. Some of the most interesting literary works to appear were published by the Jesuit mission press. Religious works made up the largest category, but the press also published miscellaneous literary forms including a translation of *Aesop's Fables*.

THE INTERNATIONAL DIMENSION OF THE PERIOD

The pronounced international flavor of Azuchi-Momoyama was brought about largely by the novel presence of European traders and Catholic missionaries. For the first time, Japan came directly into contact with European civilization. This cosmopolitan epoch extends from 1563—the year when the Kyūshū baron Ōmura Sumitada, seeking to cement his ties with the Portuguese traders, accepted baptism from the Jesuit missionaries whom they supported, thus becoming the first of the Christian daimyō—to 1597, when the Twenty-Six Martyrs of Japan were crucified on Hideyoshi's orders in the first bloody persecution of Christianity.

In 1582, four Japanese Christian boys were sent to Rome for an audience with Pope Gregory XIII on behalf of the Christian daimyō in Kyūshū (mission to Europe of 1582). However, during their absence Hideyoshi issued the anti-Christian edict, and they were not able to publicize their experience when they returned in 1590.

　16世紀末には、日本人は東アジアの大陸に
向かって、活発な行動を開始した。1590年代に
は、失敗に終わった、秀吉の朝鮮での軍事行動
がある。秀吉は1592年から1598年までの期間、
朝鮮で戦ったが（文禄・慶長の役）、この朝鮮侵
略の試みは秀吉の死で終止符を打たれた。日
本人の海外進出の野心は、朱印船貿易の制度化
によって、より平和的な経路に方向転換された。

　日本の商人は、利益を求めて、インドシナ、シ
ャム（現タイ）、それに香料群島（現マルク諸島）
にまで活動範囲を広げ、多くの日本人町も築か
れた。しかし、1620年代と1630年代には、徳川
幕府が外国人の日本滞在と日本人の海外渡航
の両方に、ますます厳しい制限を加えた。1639
年以降、日本は少数の外国と厳しく制約された
外交ならびに通商関係を維持したにすぎない。
　安土桃山時代という外向的な時代の後に続
くのは、長い内向の時代である。

The end of the sixteenth century saw the beginning of an extraordinary burst of Japanese activities directed toward mainland East Asia. The 1590s witnessed Hideyoshi's abortive military adventure in Korea. He fought in Korea between 1592 and 1598 (Bunroku Keichō no Eki; invasions of Korea in 1592 and 1597); the invasions ended upon Hideyoshi's death. Japanese ambitions for overseas ventures were thereupon redirected into a more peaceful channel with the systematization of the vermilion-seal ship trade.

Japanese traders were ranging as far as Indochina, Siam, and the Spice Islands in search of profits and many Japanese communities were established there. In the 1620s and 1630s, however, the Tokugawa shogunate was to apply ever stricter controls both on foreigners resident in Japan and on Japanese voyaging abroad. From 1639, Japan maintained only a highly restricted form of diplomatic and commercial relations with a few foreign nations.

Azuchi-Momoyama, an extroverted period of history, was followed by a long era of introversion.

江戸時代

（1600〜1868年）

江戸時代は徳川時代とも呼ばれ、徳川家康が関ヶ原の戦いで最大の敵を破った1600年から、1868年の明治維新までである。

　江戸時代は日本史上画期的な時代の1つで、日本が国内、国外を問わず、戦争から解放され、2世紀余りの平和を享受したという際立った事実がそれを示している。権威主義的な施政と鎖国政策にもかかわらず、日本はこの時代に、政治、社会、経済、それに文化の面で、重要な変化を経験した。

　江戸時代には、強力な幕府の支配下で、武家の領主（大名）による地方統治の体制が安定する。武士という自意識の強い支配階級は政府の機能を全面的に独占した。徳川幕府は武士の下に、平民を分類する階級を定めた。特に重要な階級は、百姓と町人である。武士階級はほとんど全員が農村地帯を離れて領主の城下町に住んだために、都市の急速な、しかも大幅な成長を促した。

Tokugawa Ieyasu
(1543–1616). The
worrior chieftain who,
outwitting many of his
major contemporaries
and outliving and
outprocreating the
rest, survived Japan's
late-16th-century wars
of unification.

徳川政権の確立

徳川家康は、関ヶ原の戦いで、全国の大名に対する軍事的優位を決定的なものにしてから3年後の1603年、天皇から将軍に任ぜられた。家康が築いた政治体制は幕藩体制と呼ばれ、この体制下での施政は2つの政治機構を通じて行われた。将軍の統治機関、幕府と、大名の領地、藩である。

Edo Period

(1600–1868)

The Edo period, also called the Tokugawa period, dates from 1600, when Ieyasu defeated his principal rivals in the Battle of Sekigahara, to 1868, the year of the Meiji Restoration.

One of the major epochs of Japanese history, the Edo period is distinguished by the fact that for more than two centuries Japan enjoyed freedom from warfare at home and abroad. Despite authoritarian administration and a policy of "National Seclusion," Japan experienced significant political, social, economic, and cultural change during this period.

The Edo period witnessed the stabilization of the system of local rule by military lords (*daimyō*) under strong shogunal authority. A self-conscious ruling class of *samurai* monopolized all functions of government. Under them, the Tokugawa shogunate defined separate classes of commoners, the farmer (*hyakushō*) and the townsman (*chōnin*) being the most important. Almost the entire samurai class left the countryside to reside in the castle towns of their daimyō lords, stimulating a rapid and widespread growth of cities.

ESTABLISHMENT OF THE TOKUGAWA POWER STRUCTURE

Tokugawa Ieyasu received the title of shōgun from the emperor in 1603, three years after achieving military supremacy over all the daimyō of Japan in the decisive Battle of Sekigahara. The political system created by Ieyasu was the *bakuhan* system (shogunate and domain system), under which government functioned through two political mechanisms: the *bakufu* or shogunate, and the *han* or daimyō domain.

　家康は忠誠心の厚い家来の一部を大名とし
て全国に配置し、最終的に145家からなる譜代
大名といわれる大名のグループにとりたてた。
親藩と呼ばれる第2の範疇の大名は、徳川家の
血筋を引くグループで、最終的に23家が残った。
残りは、関ヶ原の戦い以前に徳川方について生
き延びたか、敵方について戦ったにもかかわら
ず、家康によって家の断絶を容赦された大名で
ある。彼らは外様大名と呼ばれ、18世紀末には
98家ほどあった。徳川家そのものも、この体制
の強力な一員だった。将軍は全国の知行高、推
定3,000万石のうち、推定400万石を直轄地「天
領」として領有し、さらに300万石を将軍直属の
家来「旗本」の知行として確保していた。

徳川政権の正当化：支配構造

徳川将軍は軍事政権の最高権力者として、大名
や寺社の行動を規制し、国の軍事ならびに財政
政策を定めて、全国に広範な支配力を及ぼし
た。対外的にも、他国との交渉、キリスト教の禁
止、貿易の管理、日本人の海外旅行の制限は、
将軍が自らの権限として行った。将軍の最も重
要な権力は、国土の究極的な領有権であった。

　将軍の最も効果的な管理方式は、参勤交代
制度である。この制度によって、1630年代以降、
すべての大名とその家族が江戸城の近くに屋敷
を構え、定期的に将軍に敬意を表することを義
務づけられた。

　将軍が各藩の問題に直接干渉することはまれ

Ieyasu set out some of his loyal retainers as daimyō, creating a class known as *fudai* (hereditary vassals), a group that eventually numbered 145 houses. A second category of daimyō were the *shimpan* (collateral or cadet daimyō), made up of lineages related to the Tokugawa house, of whom twenty-three eventually survived. The remaining daimyō were men who had either survived Sekigahara by joining the Tokugawa side before the battle or who had been spared extinction by Ieyasu despite having fought on the losing side. These daimyō, known as *tozama* (outside lords), numbered some ninety-eight at the end of the eighteenth century. The Tokugawa house itself constituted a major power bloc. Of Japan's estimated total of 30 million *koku* of land, the shōgun directly held granary lands (known as *tenryō*) assessed at some 4 million *koku*, while another 3 million *koku* were held by the shōgun's enfeoffed *hatamoto* (bannermen).

LEGITIMATION OF THE TOKUGAWA REGIME: THE AUTHORITY STRUCTURE

As chief of the military estate, the Tokugawa shōgun exercised broad national authority, regulating affairs among the daimyō and religious bodies and setting national military and fiscal policy. In foreign affairs, too, the shōgun assumed the rights to negotiate with other states, stamp out Christianity, control trade, and restrict travel by Japanese. The most important of the shōgun's powers was that of ultimate proprietorship of the country's land.

The shōgun's most effective control device was the *sankin kōtai*, or alternate attendance requirement. From the 1630s this practice obliged all daimyō and their families to establish residences near Edo Castle and pay regular homage to the shōgun.

The shōgun rarely interfered directly in the internal

だったが、将軍は大名たちにいくつかの基本政
策と規定に従うことを厳しく要求した。このこと
は、武家諸法度のなかの「全国のすべての問題
を江戸の法律に則して処理しなければならな
い」という言葉で明確に示されている。

幕藩体制：中央と地方の行政

幕府の政務は2つの役職によって統轄された。
中級の譜代大名のなかから任命される5人ある
いは6人の上級評議員（老中）は、幕政全体を統
轄する、幕府政治の中枢の行政会議を構成し
た。もう1つ、3人ないし5人の下級評議員（若年
寄）が構成する会議は、幕府の内部問題を管轄
した。

　幕府の重要な機能を司る役職は老中の支配
下に置かれた。重要都市の長官（町奉行）、財
務長官（勘定奉行）、大坂城の政務代行者（城
代）、京都担当長官（京都所司代）、監察長官
（大目付）などである。その全てが譜代大名か旗
本だった。

　農村部の支配と年貢徴収の基本単位になっ
たのは村である。村は年貢を課せられた農民
（百姓）とその小作人と下人労働者によって構成
された。村の自治は百姓に任された。村にはそ
れぞれの長（名主あるいは庄屋）、村長の補佐
役（組頭）、それに百姓の代表（百姓代）がいた。

幕藩体制：社会構造と階級政策

徳川政権は公的な目的のために、中国にあった
4民（士農工商）の概念を取り入れ、身分制度を
法によって定めた。徳川幕府の法はそのほかに

affairs of the domains. However, he did insist upon strict conformity to certain basic policies and regulations. This was made clear in the Buke Shohatto (Laws for the Military Houses), which stated that "throughout the country all matters are to be carried out in accordance with the laws of Edo."

THE BAKUHAN SYSTEM: CENTRAL AND LOCAL ADMINISTRATION

The shōgun worked through two boards of retainers. A group of five or six senior councillors (*rōjū*), appointed from among mid-ranking *fudai* daimyō, made up a high administrative council with authority over matters of nationwide scope. A second board, consisting of three to five junior councillors (*wakadoshiyori*), had charge of the shogunate's internal affairs.

The most important functional officers of the shogunate were placed under the senior councillors. These included the commissioners of major cities (*machi bugyō*), the commissioners of finance (*kanjō bugyō*), the keeper (*jōdai*) of Ōsaka Castle, the Kyōto deputy (Kyōto *shoshidai*), the inspectors general (*ōmetsuke*), and lesser officers. All were either *fudai* daimyō or bannermen.

Villages functioned as basic units of rural control and taxation. They were composed of taxpaying farmers (*hyakushō*) and their tenants and dependent workers. It was left to the *hyakushō* to maintain village self-management. Each village had its headman (*nanushi* or *shōya*), assistant headman (*kumigashira*), and *hyakushō* representative (*hyakushōdai*).

THE BAKUHAN SYSTEM: SOCIAL STRUCTURE AND CLASS POLICY

Tokugawa legislation engineered the class structure by adopting for official purposes a four-class concept that had originated in China (*shi-nō-kō-shō*; warrior-farmer-artisan-

も、朝廷に仕える貴族階級（公家）、僧侶と尼僧、それに最下層の賤民視された人々など、いくつかの社会的グループの存在を認めている。

　身分制は、社会的グループそれぞれの身分に寄せられる期待と、生活のスタイルを、非常に異なるものにした。武士の大部分は城下町の城の周囲の石垣と濠で囲まれた特別区域に居住し、武官あるいは文官として官僚的な任務を果たす以外に道がなかった。町人は都市の一部の区域に居住を制限され、その低い身分にふさわしい姿勢を保ちつつ、武士にサービスを提供することを期待された。農民はその定義通り農村で生活し、勤勉と節約を厳しく諭された。

　徳川政権の法は儒教の社会的概念に負うところが大きい。儒教の唱導する基本的道徳、忠と孝は、保守的な概念で、現行の社会的ならびに政治的秩序を支えた。

外国との接触の制限

家康は、キリスト教は政治的に徳川政権を脅かしかねない、という疑念を強め、1612年、最初の禁教令を発した。家康の跡を継いだ徳川秀忠と徳川家光は、この政策を強化し、1637〜38年の島原の乱で、幕府は極端なまでの反キリスト教的措置を取るに至る。全国すべての家は地域の寺（檀那寺）に登録を義務づけられ、毎年、キリシタンでないことを示す証拠を提出しなければならなかった。

　一方、外国貿易の規制もそれに並行して行われ、朝鮮との貿易は対馬に限られた。1635年、日本人の海外渡航と在外日本人の帰国が禁止された（海外渡航禁止令）。1639年、ポルトガル

merchant). Tokugawa law recognized a number of other social groups, such as the court aristocracy (*kuge*), priests and nuns (*sō* and *ni*), and outcasts.

The legal separation of classes gave rise to quite different expectations and styles of life for each segment of society. Most samurai lived in towns, within the walled and moated enclosures surrounding their lords' castles, and were restricted to military and civil-bureaucratic service. *Chōnin* were confined to certain sections of town and were expected to provide services for the samurai while maintaining a posture befitting their low status. Farmers by definition lived in villages where they were admonished to work hard and live frugally.

Tokugawa law relied heavily on the social concepts of Confucianism. The basic moral concepts advocated by Confucianism—loyalty (*chū*) and filial piety (*kō*)—were conservative and supportive of the existing social and political order.

RESTRICTION OF FOREIGN CONTACT

With a growing suspicion that Christianity was politically dangerous to his regime, Ieyasu issued his first anti-Christian edict in 1612. His two immediate successors, Tokugawa Hidetada and Tokugawa Iemitsu, intensified this policy, and the Shimabara Uprising of 1637–38 pushed the shogunate to its most extreme anti-Christian measures. All Japanese families had to register at a local temple (*dannadera*) and give evidence annually that they were not contaminated by Christianity.

Meanwhile, regulation of foreign trade moved in parallel. The Korean trade was confined to Tsushima. In 1635, Japanese nationals were forbidden to travel abroad or return home from overseas (Prohibitions of Foreign Voyages). In 1639,

船の来航が禁止され、オランダ人と中国人だけ
が長崎での交易を許された。こうして日本は2世
紀余りの鎖国の時代に入り、その間、幕藩体制
下の「偉大な平和」は、国内からも海外からも、
戦争によって乱されることがなかった。

幕藩体制の変遷

最初の3代の将軍は、その体制の支配機構と行
政組織を完成させ、幕府側に有利な力の均衡
をはかるために、心血を注いだ。しかし、1651
年、家光の跡を継いだ子の徳川家綱は病弱な
10歳の少年でしかなかった。彼の時代には、幕
政の大部分を老中が担い、その結果、幕府の
利益よりも、譜代大名の利益を反映する幕政の
スタイルが生まれた。

　5代将軍徳川綱吉は、老中の影響力を避ける
ために側近を重用した。綱吉は寵臣柳沢吉保
を重用し、側用人による統治の先例になった。8
代将軍徳川吉宗は、政治体制ならびに財政の
精力的な改革に着手した。これは享保の改革
と呼ばれ、江戸時代の3大改革の最初になる。

　日本は1780年代に、多くの決定的な国内問題
に直面した。1782年から1787年には、凶作によ
って、諸国で大飢饉が起きた(天明の飢饉)。江
戸の街は暴動(打ちこわし)で揺さぶられた。11
代将軍徳川家斉は幼少であったために、老中首
座の松平定信に補佐された。江戸時代の2つ目
の改革、寛政の改革は松平定信が行ったが、そ
の内容は保守的なものであった。

　1790年代までは、幕府は主に国内問題に対

Portuguese ships were excluded from Japanese ports, and only the Dutch and Chinese were allowed to trade at Nagasaki. Thus Japan entered its period of National Seclusion that was to last more than two centuries, during which no warfare either domestic or foreign disturbed the "Great Peace" under the *bakuhan* regime.

EVOLUTION OF THE BAKUHAN STATE

The first three shōguns perfected the control mechanisms and the administrative machinery of their regimes and made strenuous efforts to increase the balance of power in favor of the shogunate. Then, in 1651, Iemitsu was succeeded by his son Tokugawa Ietsuna, a fragile youth of 10. Under him, policy was made largely by the senior councillors, resulting in a style of shogunal rule that reflected the interests of the *fudai* daimyō more than the central interests of the shōgun.

The fifth shōgun, Tokugawa Tsunayoshi, relied heavily on his private officials to circumvent the senior councillors. Tsunayoshi's reliance on his favorite, Yanagisawa Yoshiyasu, set an example of rule through the grand chamberlain (*sobayōnin*). The eighth shōgun, Tokugawa Yoshimune, embarked on a strenuous program of bureaucratic and financial reforms. Known as the Kyōhō Reforms, these were the first of three major reform attempts made during the period.

The country faced many critical domestic problems by the 1780s. Between 1782 and 1787, crop failures caused famine conditions in much of Japan (Temmei Famine). Edo was shaken by urban riots. The eleventh shōgun, Tokugawa Ienari, being a minor, was placed under the guidance of a new chief shogunate officer, Matsudaira Sadanobu. Sadanobu is credited with carrying out the second of the conservative reform programs, the Kansei Reforms.

Up to the 1790s, the shogunate's problems had been

処するだけだったが、19世紀の初めには、ロシアやイギリスの船が日本の海域に現れ、日本は外国の脅威にも直面しなければならなかった。

　1841年、家斉の死後、老中筆頭の水野忠邦は、3大改革の最後になる最も急進的な天保の改革に着手した。水野の計画は幕府の経済的ならびに政治的な地位を向上させることを目的としていたが、広範な人々の反感を買い、まもなく水野は失脚する。その跡を継いだ老中首座の阿部正弘は水野の新政策の大部分を撤回した。

　とはいえ、1853年、マシュウ・ペリー提督によって引き起こされた危機に直面させられたのは、この阿部正弘である。彼の2つの決定が徳川政権の終わりを告げた。彼は先ず、アメリカの開港要求にどう対処するべきか、について、外様を含む全ての大名の意見を求めた。これによって外交政策は幕府の一存で決定するという、幕府の特権を放棄する。そしてさらに、大名に彼ら自身の沿岸警備体制を奨励することによって、大名の軍事力を制限する幕府の権限を弱める。鎖国の終わりと、軍事技術の進歩によって、幕府は全国支配の能力を失い、ついに、徳川政権は終わる。

江戸時代の経済と文化の発展

江戸時代の社会に最大の影響を及ぼした変化は疑いもなく、都市の発展である。16世紀半ばに地方統治の単位として統一された大名の藩の出現と、武士の農村からの移住は、たちまち全国各地に城下町を生み出した。最大の城下町江戸の人口は、18世紀半ばまでに100万人近く

Matthew Calbraith Perry
(1794–1858). This US naval officer led the 1853–54 expedition that reopened Japan's diplomatic and commercial relations with the Western world.

mainly domestic, but by the beginning of the nineteenth century, with the appearance of Russian and British ships in Japanese waters, Japan faced an external threat as well.

In 1841, upon the death of Ienari, Mizuno Tadakuni, chief of the senior councillors, initiated the Tempō Reforms, the last and most drastic of the three reforms. Mizuno's program was intended to improve the economic and political positions of the shogunate, but he managed to antagonize a wide array of people and was soon forced to resign. His successor as head of the senior councillors, Abe Masahiro, rescinded most of his initiatives.

It was Abe, however, who had to face the crisis created by the arrival of U.S. Commodore Matthew Perry in 1853. Abe did two things that signaled the end of Tokugawa power. By soliciting all daimyō, including *tozama*, for opinions on how to handle the American request for the opening of Japanese ports, he abandoned the shogunal prerogative of determining foreign policy unilaterally. By encouraging daimyō to build up their own coastal defenses, he weakened the shōgun's power to control their military strength. With the end of Japan's isolation and the advance of military technology, the shogunate lost its ability to assert national authority, ultimately bringing the Tokugawa regime to an end.

ECONOMIC AND CULTURAL DEVELOPMENTS OF THE PERIOD

The most dramatic change to affect Edo society was without question the spread of city life. With the appearance in the mid-sixteenth century of the unified daimyō domains and the movement of the samurai off the land, regional castle towns sprang up rapidly throughout Japan. By the end of the eighteenth century, Edo, the greatest of the castle towns and the

なり、大坂と京都にはそれぞれ30万人が生活し
ていた。

　武士は軍事的な任務から、文官として官僚的
な任務に移り、教養豊かな都会人になった。彼
らが強調したのは精神修養と武士道の高揚で
あるが、江戸時代の武士が真に独創的な貢献
をしたのは、儒教の伝統に根を下ろす実用的な
学問の分野であった。

　都市化した武士の生活の充実は、都市化し
た商業ならびにサービスを提供する、町人の台
頭を伴った。

　商業的な富と町人人口の増加は、特色のあ
る文化をもつ町人社会を生んだ。豪商、三井、
住友、鴻池は現代まで存続している。

　新しいブルジョワ文化（町人文化）は、元禄時
代（1688〜1704年）に京都と大坂で最初の開花
期を迎えた。近松門左衛門の浄瑠璃や歌舞伎、
井原西鶴の浮世草子、菱川師宣の浮世絵、そ
れに松尾芭蕉の紀行文や俳諧などに代表さ
れる。

　西洋の学問と科学的な研究は、鎖国政策に
もかかわらず日本に浸透し、とりわけ1720年に
徳川吉宗が洋書の輸入を解禁し、公式の通訳
以外にもオランダ語を学ぶ機会を与えてからは、
その動きが強まった。19世紀の初期には、蘭学
あるいは洋学がかなり広範に行われている。

　1800年以降、多くの日本人は新しい学問、国
学に心を引かれた。この日本の伝統に対する

seat of government, had a population of nearly 1 million, while Ōsaka and Kyōto each had some 300,000 inhabitants.

The samurai made the transition from military duty to civil-bureaucratic service, becoming literate, cultured, and urbanized. Stress was placed on spiritual training and the cultivation of *bushidō*, or the Way of the Samurai. However, it was in the field of secular scholarship that the samurai of the Edo period made their truly original contribution. The main body of such scholarship was rooted in the Confucian tradition.

The maturation of urbanized samurai life was accompanied by the rise of an urbanized commercial and service class, the *chōnin*.

Commercial wealth and a growing *chōnin* population gave rise to a bourgeois society with its own cultural style. The greatest of the merchant houses, the Mitsui, Sumitomo, and Kōnoike, have continued into modern times.

The main elements of the emerging bourgeois culture (*chōnin bunka*) were brought to their first flowering in Kyōto and Ōsaka during the Genroku era (1688–1704). Such were the *jōruri* and *kabuki* plays of Chikamatsu Monzaemon, *Ukiyo-zōshi* of Ihara Saikaku, *Ukiyo-e* of Hishikawa Moronobu, and the poetic essays and *haiku* of Matsuo Bashō.

Despite the National Seclusion policy, knowledge of Western scholarship and scientific inquiry managed to filter into Japan, particularly after 1720 when Tokugawa Yoshimune lifted the ban on the importation of foreign books and made it possible for persons other than official interpreters to learn Dutch. By the early nineteenth century, Dutch studies (Rangaku) and Western studies (Yōgaku) had become fairly widespread.

After 1800, many Japanese were attracted to an emerging school of National Learning (Kokugaku). This interest in

関心は、国粋的な面と宗教的な面を併せ持ち、とりわけ神道の伝統への復帰を唱えた平田篤胤の著作にはその傾向が強い。神道のイデオロギー的な側面の復活は、日本の危機にあって、多くの日本人に精神的なよりどころを与えた。そして、尊皇攘夷のスローガンのもとでの、外国の脅威に対する強力で、保守的な反応の支柱になった。

幕末：徳川政権の終わり

幕府は外国の圧力に屈し、1853年から1860年にかけて伝統的な政策を放棄し、いくつかの港を外国船に開放した（開国）。そして1858年には、朝廷の反対にもかかわらず、列強との通商協定（安政の5か国条約）に調印して、外国に自由貿易を認めていた。しかし、日本側には、まだその準備が整っていなかった。1860年の井伊直弼の暗殺（桜田門外の変）は、この事態に終止符を打った。続いて、幕府と大名が天皇のもとで朝廷に協力する公武合体が試みられる。最後の将軍徳川慶喜は、公武合体のための究極の手段として、1867年、連合政権に道を譲るために、辞任を申し出た（大政奉還）。

　しかし、倒幕の動きはすでに勢いを増していた。2つの外様の大藩、薩摩と長州は若い活動家の武士を通じて同盟関係に入り、さらに朝廷の重臣とも同盟した。1868年1月、討幕派は天皇を擁して、天皇の詔として、王政復古の宣言を発表した。将軍は出し抜かれたのである。徳川方の軍勢はこの情勢に抵抗を試みたが、薩

Japanese tradition took on both nationalistic and religious dimensions, especially in the work of Hirata Atsutane, who called for a return to Shintō tradition. Revival of the ideological features of Shintō provided many Japanese with a sense of cultural security amidst the emerging sense of crisis. It laid the basis for the powerful conservative reaction to the foreign threat under the slogan Revere the Emperor, Expel the Barbarians (*sonnō jōi*).

BAKUMATSU: THE END OF THE TOKUGAWA REGIME

Between 1853 and 1860, the shogunate, unable to resist foreign pressures, abandoned its traditional policy and opened a number of ports to foreign ships (Opening of Japan). In 1858, by signing trade agreements (Ansei Commercial Treaties) with the foreign powers despite imperial disapproval, it resigned itself to free foreign intercourse. But the country was not ready to go along. The assassination in 1860 of Ii Naosuke (Sakuradamongai Incident) brought this phase to an end. There followed an effort to create a coalition government in which the shogunate and daimyō would work together with court nobles under the emperor. In a final effort at conciliation, the last shōgun, Tokugawa Yoshinobu, offered to resign in late 1867 to make way for a coalition government (Taisei Hōkan; Return of Political Rule to the Emperor).

Already, however, an anti-Tokugawa movement was gathering momentum. The two large *tozama* domains of Satsuma and Chōshū were drawn into alliance by young activist samurai and allied with key figures at the imperial court. In January 1868 this group captured the emperor and declared in his name a restoration of imperial rule (Ōsei Fukko). The shōgun had been outmaneuvered. Tokugawa forces made an

摩藩、長州藩、土佐藩の軍勢は自らを官軍と宣
言して、徳川方を京都の近くで打ち破った。将
軍は官位を剥奪され、所領を没収された。新政
府と天皇はその年に江戸に入り、幕藩体制を支
えた諸制度を次々に撤廃した。

attempt to resist this turn of events, but troops from the domains of Satsuma, Chōshū, and Tosa proclaimed themselves an imperial army and routed the Tokugawa forces near Kyōto. The former shōgun was declared a rebel and his lands confiscated. Within a year the new government and the emperor had moved to Edo, where in quick succession the main pillars of the *bakuhan* system were pulled down.

明治時代

（1868〜1912年）

明治天皇の治世で、日本の近代の始まり。明治時代は1868年10月23日、16歳の天皇睦仁がその治世の年号として明治を選んだときに始まったが、天皇による王政復古が宣言されたその年の1月3日以降を明治時代に含める。1912年7月30日の明治天皇の死によって終わる。明治時代は徳川幕府の崩壊と明治維新に伴う広範な改革とともに始まった。日本は明治時代に、孤立状態から脱出して世界の列強に加わると同時に、封建国家から近代的な工業国に生まれ変わる。

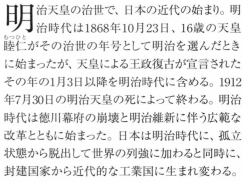

Emperor Meiji
(1852–1912). Succeeding
to the throne in 1867 at
the age of 14, Emperor
Meiji became the
symbolic focus for the
movement to overthrow
the Tokugawa
shogunate.

封建制度の廃止

明治政府は、薩摩藩と長州藩との同盟として始まった。薩摩と長州は、土佐と肥前の支援を受けて、徳川幕府を打倒した陰の力である。誕生したばかりの明治政府は、1868年1月から1869年6月まで、旧幕府軍と反政府派の諸藩を相手に、戊辰戦争を戦った。江戸は1868年、東京と改名され、新しい首都に指定された。

　明治政府は支配力を確立し、秩序の回復をはかるために、その新秩序が正義と機会を重んじる秩序であることを伝えて、国民を安心させようとした。その理想は、1868年4月6日、天皇が公布した五箇条の御誓文として具体的に示されている。五箇条の御誓文は、先ず審議機関を設置して、全ての問題を公的な討論によって決定すること、また、過去の悪弊を撤廃することを、約束していた。後者は封建制度廃止の決意を意味している。

Meiji Period

(1868–1912)

The reign of Emperor Meiji and the beginning of Japan's modern period. It began on 23 October 1868, when the sixteen-year-old emperor Mutsuhito selected the era name Meiji ("Enlightened Rule") for his reign. Extended retroactively to 3 January, when the restoration of direct imperial rule had been proclaimed, it ended with the emperor's death on 30 July 1912. The period commenced with the collapse of the Tokugawa shogunate and the sweeping reforms attendant upon the Meiji Restoration. The Meiji period saw Japan's transformation from a feudal polity into a modern industrial state, along with its emergence from isolation into the ranks of major world powers.

THE ABOLITION OF FEUDALISM

The Meiji regime began as an alliance between Satsuma and Chōshū, the two domains behind the overthrow of the Tokugawa shogunate, supported by Tosa and Hizen. From January 1868 to June 1869, the nascent Meiji state fought the Boshin Civil War against fragmented Tokugawa forces and dissident domains. Edo was renamed Tōkyō in 1868 and designated as the new national capital.

As it attempted to assert control and restore order, the Meiji government sought to reassure its subjects that this new order would be one of justice and opportunity, aspirations embodied in the Charter Oath issued by the emperor on 6 April 1868. The Charter Oath promised, among other things, that deliberative assemblies would be established and all matters decided by public discussion and that evil customs of the past would be abandoned, this last implying a commitment to abolish feudalism.

　御誓文で述べられ、さらに1868年公布の明治
政府の組織法(政体書)に明記された「審議機
関」と「公的な討論」を実現しようとする初期の
試みもあったが、明治政府はまもなく、最高執政
官(太政官)が支配権を握る権威主義的な構造
へと逆行する。その後の改革と新制度の導入
は、明治維新の指導者である薩摩、長州、土佐、
それに佐賀出身の若手の武士の先導で進めら
れた。

　1869年、4人の重要な大名が彼らの説得に応じ、
それぞれの土地(版図)と人民(戸籍)に対する支
配権を天皇に返上した(版籍奉還)。他の大名も
これにならった。そしてその全員が朝廷によって、
以前の所領の知事に任命された。しかし朝廷は
1871年、各藩の知事を解任し、藩を統合して、近
代的な組織の県を設置する(廃藩置県)。

　1871年から1873年にかけて18か月間、明治
政府の指導者の多くが、岩倉遣外使節団の一
員として、アメリカとヨーロッパを旅行した。西洋
の文明に触れて、改革の優先順位を考え直した
人が少なくない。

　封建的な藩制度と封建的な課税制度の廃止
は、新しい税制を必要とした。1873年の土地調
査の後、平均的な生産性から地価が算定され、
新しい地租は地価の3パーセントと定められた。
1873年から1881年の地租改正が及ぼした広範
な変化は、農村の反発を招いた。

　いまや中央政府は教育と防衛の全責任を負
わなければならなかった。1872年に公布された
学制は、国民全員の読み書き能力をその目標
とした。1870年から1880年には、日本の近代化

There were early attempts to implement the "assemblies" and "public discussion" mentioned in the Charter Oath, notably in the Constitution of 1868 (Seitaisho), but before long the regime reverted to a more authoritarian structure dominated by the Grand Council of State (Dajōkan). Thereafter reform and innovation proceeded from the initiative of key Restoration leaders from Satsuma, Chōshū, Tosa, and Saga, who were younger *samurai*.

In 1869, four major *daimyō* were persuaded to relinquish their domain registers to the court (*hanseki hōkan*). Other daimyō followed suit. All were appointed governors of their former domains by the court, but in 1871 the court dismissed its daimyō governors and consolidated their domains into more rationally structured prefectures (*haihan chiken*; establishment of prefectural system).

For eighteen months from 1871 to 1873, a large part of the Meiji leadership toured America and Europe as part of the Iwakura mission. Exposure to the West changed the priorities of many.

Abolishing feudal domains and feudal dues necessitated a new system of taxation. After land surveys in 1873, average productivity was capitalized to produce an estimated market value of land, and the new national land tax was set at 3 percent of this assessment. The sweeping changes of the Land Tax Reform of 1873–1881 aroused resistance in the countryside.

The central government now had to shoulder full responsibility for education and defense. The Education Order of 1872 set as its goal universal literacy. Several thousand foreign teachers and advisers (*oyatoi gaikokujin*; foreign

を支援するために、数千人の外国人教師と顧問
が政府によって雇い入れられた（明治時代のお
雇い外国人）。

西洋の軍隊の視察と、維新戦争で一般市民
による軍隊（奇兵隊）を活用した経験は、政府に
国民軍の重要性を認識させた。1872年、政府
は山県有朋の考案による徴兵制度を発表した。
1873年発布の徴兵令は、3年間の兵役と4年間
の予備役を課したが、広範な免除条項を含んで
いた。

武士階級はその存在理由を失い、徐々に廃止
された。1873年、岩倉遣外使節団の帰国後、政
府は武士の俸給である家禄に課税する決定を
し、最終的に家禄制度を廃止する（秩禄処分）。

明治維新の実現に功績のあった諸藩出身の
武士たちは、期待が大きかっただけに、失望し
た。1874年から1876年にかけて、士族の反乱が
全国各地で起こっている。新政府にとって最大
の試練は、人望の厚い西郷隆盛が反乱軍を指
揮した1877年の西南戦争だった。

「日常生活の西洋化」。近代的な中央集権国
家の基礎を築くための一連の政策は、「富国強
兵」のスローガンのもとで実施された。それに平
行して、一般市民の啓蒙運動が「文明開化」の
スローガンのもとで進められた。政府は人々に
髷を切ることを奨励し（断髪令、1871年）、刀を
帯びることを禁止したのである（廃刀令、1876
年）。新政府は電報（1870年）と郵便（1871年）の
事業を開始し、鉄道の建設に着手し（1872年）、
さらに太陽暦を採用した（1873年）。

Meiji Enlighten-ment The introduction of Western music was encouraged by the government.

employees of the Meiji period) were hired to assist Japan in its quest for modernization in the 1870s and 1880s.

Observation of Western armies and experience with commoner militias (Kiheitai; "Irregular Militia") during the Restoration convinced the government of the importance of a mass army. In 1872, the government announced a system of military conscription devised by Yamagata Aritomo. The Conscription Ordinance of 1873 called for three years of active service and four years in the reserves, but provided for liberal exceptions.

Deprived of its reason for being, the samurai class was phased out. After the Iwakura mission's return in 1873, the government decided to begin taxing samurai stipends and ultimately to eliminate them (*chitsuroku shobun*).

Samurai from the Restoration domains, where expectations had been highest, were bitterly disappointed. Samurai staged a series of revolts across the country from 1874 to 1876. The hardest test for the new government, however, came with the Satsuma Rebellion of 1877, led by the widely admired Saigō Takamori.

The Westernization of daily life. A series of policies to establish the foundation of a modern centralized state were implemented under the slogan "A Rich Country and a Strong Military." In parallel with this, the government also carried out a movement to educate the general populace, under the slogan "Civilization and Enlightenment." It encouraged people to cut off their topknots (Dampatsurei, 1871) and stop wearing swords (Haitōrei, 1876). The new government implemented telegraph (1870) and postal services (1871), started constructing railways (1872), and adopted the Gregorian calendar (1873).

制度の確立

薩摩に対する勝利は明治の新体制の基礎を固めた。しかし、反乱、暗殺、それに早世によって、新体制は西郷隆盛、大久保利通、木戸孝允など、初期のリーダーを何人か失っていた。このころから、政府の主導権は長州出身の若い伊藤博文や山県有朋、薩摩出身の財務の達人松方正義、公家の岩倉具視や西園寺公望などに受け継がれる。多くの官職が他藩の出身者はもとより、もと幕府の役人にも開かれていたが、国家の中枢で影響力を及ぼした政治家（元老）は薩摩と長州の出身者に限られていた。

「経済：松方時代」。紙幣の導入によって引き起こされたインフレの進行に直面して、新政府の財政基盤は弱かった。経費節減の運動は松方正義の指揮下で始まり、彼はそのキャリアの16年余りを、明治政府の財政に捧げた。新しい地租制度と「殖産工業政策」、通貨の管理、日本銀行の設立（1882年）、金本位制の維持は、全て彼の指揮下で行われた。松方はインフレの鎮圧をはかるために、政府の試験的な工業プロジェクトのいくつかを放棄し、戦略的な重要性をもたないプロジェクトは民間の入札者に売却した（官営事業の払い下げ）。払い下げを受けたのは、政府の指導者層に近く、共通の目的を持つ実業家たちであった。彼らは後年財閥のリーダーとして頭角を現した。

松方の財政政策、とりわけデフレ政策は、農村人口に大きな打撃を与えた。しかし、彼の政策は政府に健全な財政基盤を与え、持続的な工業生産の増大に必要な物価の安定をもたらした。

INSTITUTION BUILDING

Victory over Satsuma firmly established the Meiji regime. But revolt, assassination, and premature death had cost it some of its early leaders, men like Saigō, Ōkubo Toshimichi, and Kido Takayoshi. Henceforth, the Meiji leadership would come from such younger Chōshū men as Itō Hirobumi and Yamagata Aritomo, the Satsuma finance expert Matsukata Masayoshi, and the court nobles Iwakura Tomomi and Saionji Kimmochi. Though many positions were open to outsiders from other domains and even to Tokugawa veterans, the senior statesmen (*genrō*) came from Satsuma and Chōshū.

Economy: the Matsukata era. Faced with runaway inflation incurred by printing money, the new government was still in a precarious position. A campaign of retrenchment began under the direction of Matsukata Masayoshi, who devoted more than sixteen years of his career to Meiji finances. A new land tax and the campaign of "Increase Production and Promote Industry," management of the currency, establishment of the Bank of Japan (1882), and adherence to the gold standard were all carried out under his direction. To help put an end to inflation, Matsukata abandoned some of the government's pilot industrial projects, selling those not of strategic importance to private bidders (*kan'ei jigyō haraisage*; sale of government enterprises). Close to government leaders and sharing their goals, these men emerged as leaders of the future *zaibatsu.*

The Matsukata fiscal policy, particularly of deflation, proved hard on the agrarian sector. However, his policies placed the government on a sound financial basis and provided the stability necessary for sustained industrial growth.

　「軍隊：山県有朋」。軍部の権限の制度化は明らかに山県有朋の功績である。彼は軍の指揮機能（統帥権）を一般行政から引き離し、結果的に、軍部が独自の判断で天皇に接触する権限を強めた。山県の後継者桂太郎はドイツの軍隊の調査結果に基づいて、参謀本部制を立案した。

　山県は一連の規則を定め、最終的に1882年の軍人勅諭によって、天皇に対する絶対忠誠を強調した。そして1900年には、陸・海軍大臣を現役の大将・中将に限り任命することを提案する（軍部大臣現役武官制）。

　「憲法の起草者：伊藤博文」。明治政府は、近代的な西洋諸国の憲法による正式な国体の重要性を認め、1875年、試験的な審議機関として元老院を設置した。

　1889年の大日本帝国憲法（あるいは明治憲法）は、大部分が伊藤博文の起草による。彼はドイツの憲法理論家の影響を強く受けた。そして、新しい社会の要（かなめ）になり得るものは、皇室以外にないと考えた。1888年、憲法草案を審議し、守るために、枢密院が設置された。

　伊藤博文をはじめ彼の同僚たちは、日本の国民は時代遅れで、参政権を行使する準備はまだ整っていないと判断した。彼らはまた、日本の急進的な動きは、慎重な重りをつけた憲法ですぐにも抑制しなければならない、という考えで一致していた。さもなければ、その動きは内戦に進みかねなかったのである。この考えにそれなりの根拠があったことは、そのころに始まった自由

Military: Yamagata Aritomo. The institutionalization of military authority was preeminently the work of Yamagata Aritomo. He introduced measures that separated the military command function (*tōsuiken*) from routine administration, thereby strengthening the military's independent access to the throne. His protégé Katsura Tarō mapped out the General Staff system based on observations of the German military.

Yamagata issued a series of regulations culminating in the Imperial Rescript to Soldiers and Sailors of 1882, emphasizing absolute loyalty to the emperor. In 1900, he initiated a law that the army minister should be a general and the navy minister an admiral on the active list (*gumbu daijin gen'eki bukan sei*; active duty officers as service ministers).

Drafter of the Constitution: Itō Hirobumi. Convinced of the importance of formal constitutional structures in modern Western countries, the government in 1875 established the Genrōin as an experimental deliberative body.

The 1889 Constitution of the Empire of Japan (or Meiji Constitution) was largely the work of Itō Hirobumi. Itō was strongly influenced by German constitutional theorists. He saw the imperial house as the only possible fulcrum for a new society. To review and guard the constitution, a Privy Council was set up in 1888.

Itō and his associates regarded their countrymen as backward and ill-prepared for the exercise of political rights. They also shared the conviction that radical currents in Japan must be quickly checked by a carefully weighted charter, lest they lead to civil war, a view given substance by the burgeoning Freedom and People's Rights Movement. The leader of the Movement was Itagaki Taisuke. Back in 1874, when the government made an unpopular decision against a

民権運動が立証していた。運動のリーダーは板垣退助だった。1874年、政府が征韓論に反対の決定を下したときに、その決定に不満を抱いた土佐と佐賀出身のリーダーの多くが官職から退き、選挙によって代表を選ぶ審議機関の設立を求める運動を起こしていた。1881年、板垣は同志とともに日本で最初の全国的政党、自由党を結成した。その翌年、同じような政治組織、立憲改進党を大隈重信が結成した。

1880年代の半ばには、秩父事件など、不成功に終わったとはいえ、警戒を要する農村の暴動がいくつか起こった。そのころには、政党も一時的に解散を命じられ、政府はさらに政治活動を抑制した。政府はまた、新憲法によって、新しい帝国議会の下院（衆議院）に代表を送る権利を認め、政治への参加をある程度許せば、反対派を永久的に懐柔できるものと期待した。

立憲政体

明治憲法は1889年、天皇からの贈り物として、ようやく発布された。明治憲法は天皇の完全な主権を認め、天皇は「神聖であって、冒すことができない」と宣言した：軍の統帥、講和、宣戦、衆議院の解散と選挙を命じる権限を天皇に認めたのである。政治の実権は行政府にあったが、行政府の権限は天皇の特権を侵害しないように、明確にされなかった。

とはいえ、憲法が一般市民の政治参加に向かっての一歩前進になったことは確かである。衆議院は、納税額による資格を満たした約50万人の有権者が選出する議員によって構成される立法機関だった。予算の成立には、帝国議会の承認が必要とされた。

punitive attack on Korea, many Tosa and Saga leaders had withdrawn from the Meiji regime to issue a call for an elective assembly. In 1881, Itagaki and others founded the Jiyūtō (Liberal Party), Japan's first national political party. The next year, the Rikken Kaishintō (Constitutional Reform Party), a similar political organization, was founded by Ōkuma Shigenobu.

In the mid-1880s, there were several unsuccessful but alarming rural outbreaks such as the Chichibu Incident. By the middle of the decade, with parties temporarily disbanded, the government further restrained political activity. It also hoped that the new constitution would co-opt the dissidents permanently by granting them limited participation in government through membership in the lower house of the new Imperial Diet.

CONSTITUTIONAL GOVERNMENT

The Meiji Constitution was finally promulgated in 1889 as a gift from the sovereign. The constitution invested the emperor with full sovereignty, declaring him "sacred and inviolable:" he commanded the armed forces, made peace and declared war, and dissolved the lower house to call elections. Effective power lay with the executive, but executive authority was vaguely defined lest it seem to interfere with the imperial prerogative.

Yet the constitution marked a genuine step toward popular participation. The lower house of the Diet, elected by the approximately half-million voters who met tax qualifications, could initiate legislation. Diet approval was required to pass the budget.

　宮内省と内大臣は、天皇に任命権があったために権力の中枢になった。天皇自身は君臨したが、実際に統治することはなかった。

　「日清戦争、1894〜95年」。明治時代の日本は中国との戦争によって、国内政治の泥沼から、一気に愛国心を高めた。日本と中国の抗争は、朝鮮が反乱軍の鎮圧のために中国の支援を求めたことから始まった。日本は朝鮮の国王を捕らえて、日本の支援を要請することを強要し、その結果として始まった1894年から1895年の日清戦争を、近代化を必要とする朝鮮のために、時代遅れの中国を懲らしめるという、愛他主義的な行動であるかのように自認したのであった。

　日本の軍隊は全面的な勝利を納め、朝鮮の国内にあった中国の軍事力を排除して、遼東半島を占領した。下関講和会議で、日本は台湾と、2億両（テール；約3億円）という高額の賠償金と、遼東半島を要求したが、結局、ドイツ、フランス、ロシアの三国干渉によって、さらに3000万両の賠償金の追加と引き替えに遼東半島は返還しなければならなかった。日本は下関条約によって、西欧の列強と同等の特権を中国から取りつけ、そのうえさらに、条約港における企業権など、いくつかの利権を取りつけている。

日露戦争と大国の地位の獲得

日本は1850年代以来、不平等条約によって課された制約のもとで苦しんできたが、1894年、日英通商航海条約によって、治外法権と最恵国条項が1899年には終焉し、日本が自主的に関税を設定する権利も1911年には獲得できることが

The emperor's power of appointment made the Imperial Household Ministry and lord keeper of the privy seal (*naidaijin*) important bastions of power. The emperor himself reigned rather than ruled.

Sino-Japanese War, 1894–1895. From the morass of domestic politics, Meiji Japan was suddenly called to the higher ground of national unity through war with China. The two countries came to blows over Korean requests to China for help against rebels. The Japanese seized the Korean king and forced him to "request" Japan's assistance, allowing them to portray the resulting Sino-Japanese War of 1894–1895 as an altruistic action against a "backward" China on behalf of a Korea in need of "modernization."

Japan's armies were uniformly victorious, destroying Chinese military capability in Korea and seizing the Liaodong Peninsula. At the peace conference in Shimonoseki, Japan demanded the island of Taiwan, a large indemnity of 200 million taels, and the Liaodong Peninsula. But the Tripartite Intervention by Germany, France, and Russia forced retrocession of Liaodong in return for an additional 30 million taels in indemnification. By the Treaty of Shimonoseki, Japan also became heir to all privileges extracted by the West from China and gained certain additional concessions, such as the right to manufacture in treaty ports.

THE RUSSO-JAPANESE WAR AND THE RISE TO GREAT POWER STATUS

Japan had chafed under the restrictions imposed by the unequal treaties since the 1850s. The Anglo-Japanese Commercial Treaty of 1894 provided for an end to extraterritoriality and the most-favored-nation clause by 1899 and for

保証された。そのほかの列強とも、まもなく同様
の条約が締結された。

　ヨーロッパ人が中国で利権をむさぼった19世
紀末に、ロシアは日本に放棄させた遼東半島を
占有し、フランスとドイツはそれぞれ、南部と山
東半島の港を確保した。シベリア横断鉄道の完
成が近づくと、ロシアによる南満州と朝鮮北部の
永久的な支配が予想されるようになった。

　極東に同盟国を求めるイギリスと、ロシアを牽
制したい日本の利害が一致した。1902年の日
英同盟は、イギリスの艦隊による日本の保護を
約束した。1904年の初め、日本の艦隊はロシア
の太平洋艦隊を旅順で攻撃した。こうして始ま
った日露戦争は、人的ならびに金銭的に、日本
に大きな犠牲を強いたが、日本が前線に近かっ
たことと、ロシアの司令部が決断力を欠いてい
たことは、旅順と奉天会戦での日本の勝ち戦に
つながり、1905年の対馬沖の日本海海戦で、ロ
シアのバルチック艦隊を打ち破ったことは、日
本の勝利の決め手になった。

　日本はポーツマス条約によって、韓国に対す
るいっさいの指導権を認められ、南満州の租借
権をはじめ、10年前に否定された利権を回復し
て、サハリン（樺太）の南半分を獲得した。

　明治時代の最後の10年間は、日本が帝国主義
的な大国の役割を演じるために努力した時代だ
った。すでに日本の勢力圏にあった韓国は、愛
国主義者安重根による伊藤博文の暗殺の後、
1910年、正式に日本に併合された（日韓併合）。
国内政治の面では、かつて問題視された政党運

Japan's right to set its own tariffs by 1911. Similar treaties with other powers soon followed.

During the period of European concession grabbing in China at the end of the century, Russia appropriated the Liaodong Peninsula it had forced Japan to relinquish, while France and Germany secured ports in the south and in Shandong, respectively. With the Trans-Siberian Railway nearing completion, permanent Russian control of southern Manchuria and northern Korea seemed likely.

Britain's search for an ally in the Far East coincided with Japan's need to offset Russian power. The Anglo-Japanese Alliance of 1902 gave Japan the protection of the British fleet. Early in 1904, the Japanese fleet launched an attack on the Russian Pacific squadron at Port Arthur (Ryojun). The ensuing Russo-Japanese War proved immensely costly to Japan in men and money, but Japan's proximity to the fronts and indecisiveness among the Russian command brought victories at Port Arthur and in the Battle of Mukden, culminating in the destruction of the Russian Baltic fleet in the Battle of Tsushima in 1905.

By the Treaty of Portsmouth, Japan gained recognition of its paramount interests in Korea, took back the southern Manchurian leases and rights it had been denied ten years earlier, and acquired the southern half of Sakhalin (Karafuto).

The last decade of the Meiji period was dominated by Japan's efforts to assume the role of a major imperialist power. Korea, already in Japan's orbit, was formally annexed in 1910 (annexation of Korea) after a Korean patriot, An Chung Gün, assassinated Itō Hirobumi. Domestic politics saw the once-troublesome political party movement drawn into

動が体制内に組み込まれ、政友会は体制による
保護の見返りとして、帝国議会で体制を支援した。

　日本の経済は急速に成長していた。1900年
には国民総生産に占める農業生産の割合が半
分以下になり、とりわけ繊維製品などの製造業
の占める割合が着実に増大した。工業化は労
働力を都市に集中させ、都市は暴動に脅かさ
れた。明治の指導者たちは、西洋の自由主義
と急進主義の侵入を恐れ、日本の伝統的な社
会制度の維持に努力した。いまや戦争の勝利
に結びつき、近代化のシンボルであった明治天
皇は、かつてない崇高な地位にまつりあげられた。

　内務省は各行政単位内に、国家のために殉
難した人々の霊を祀る神社（招魂社）を建立し
て、土着の信仰である神道を政治に利用しよう
とした。また、政府の転覆計画を恐れて、警察
による監視体制を強化し、ついに1910年の大逆
事件を引き起こした。

文学と芸術

西洋から輸入されたイデオロギーはやがて伝統
的な美意識に影響を及ぼし、文学や芸術に広
範な変化をもたらした。口語体による文学は、二
葉亭四迷の『浮雲』で初めて完成された。代表
的な文学思潮は、1890年代に森鷗外が紹介し
たロマン主義と、後に私小説のジャンルを生む
自然主義である。夏目漱石は鷗外とともに、こ
の時代を代表する作家である。

　西洋美術に寄せられた初期の情熱はまもなく、
岡倉覚三（天心）とアーネスト・フェノロサによっ
て推奨された伝統的な美術の再評価に道を譲

the establishment, with the Seiyūkai providing parliamentary support in return for patronage.

Japan's economy was growing rapidly. By 1900, agriculture provided less than half the national product as the share of manufacturing, especially textiles, increased steadily. Industrialization concentrated labor in the cities, bringing fears of urban unrest. Worried about inroads by Western liberalism and radicalism, Meiji leaders focused on upholding Japan's traditional institutions. Emperor Meiji, now associated with success in war and always the symbol of modernization, was raised to new heights of reverence.

The Home Ministry undertook to place the native cult of Shintō at the service of the government by establishing State Shintō shrines within administrative units. Fears of subversion strengthened police surveillance and resulted in the High Treason Incident of 1910.

LITERATURE AND ART

An imported Western ideology began to affect traditional aesthetics and brought sweeping changes to its literature and art. The usage of colloquial speech was fully achieved for the first time in *Ukigumo* (Drifting Clouds) by Futabatei Shimei. Early stylistic influences on the literature were romanticism, introduced in the 1890s by Mori Ōgai, and naturalism, out of which developed the genre of the I-novel. Natsume Sōseki, along with Ōgai, are considered among the greatest writers of this period.

The initial enthusiasms for Western art soon yielded to renewed appreciation of traditional art, promoted by Okakura Kakuzō (Tenshin) and Ernest Fenollosa. Yet

った。とはいえ、洋画もやがてその本領を発揮
し、1893年には黒田清輝がフランスへの留学か
ら帰国して、洋画のリーダーになった。

Western-style painting (*yōga*) soon reasserted itself. In 1893, Kuroda Seiki returned from studies in France to become the leader of Western-style painting.

大正時代

(1912〜26年)

大正天皇の治世で、ある日本の歴史家によ
れば、「偉大な可能性の時代」である。一
部の歴史家は大正デモクラシーという用語を用い
て、この時代を政治的ならびに社会的な民主化
の始まりに結びつける。さらにまた、ほかの歴史
家は、それ以外の一連の趨勢をとらえて、1930年
代から40年代初期の特徴になる急進的なナショ
ナリズム、拡張主義、それに反自由主義の根源
は大正時代にある、と考えることもできるという。

国の指導者層の交代
明治時代の最後の10年間の妥協の政治は、
1912年から13年の大正政変によって中断され
た。この政変で1913年、第3次桂内閣が最初の
憲政擁護運動によって打倒された。

Emperor Taishō
(1879–1926). The
Taishō emperor
ascended the throne
in 1912, but lifelong
health problems
forced the appointment
of his son Hirohito as
regent in 1921.

　それから4年間は、元老が社会的地位のある
政党外の指導者を総理大臣に推薦した。しかし
現実には、どの内閣もその政策の実施には帝国
議会での政党の支持に頼らなければならず、結
果的に2大政党制度が芽生えていた。政友会と
立憲同志会（やがて憲政会として再組織される）
が交代で政治に影響力を及ぼしたのである。
1918年には、政友会の総裁原敬が元老によって
総理大臣に推薦され、それから3年間、事実上、
日本で最初の政党内閣を指揮した。

　1921年の原敬の暗殺は、国の指導権の政党
への移行を一時的に停止させたが、1924年か

Taishō Period

(1912–26)

The reign of Emperor Taishō, characterized by one Japanese historian as "an era of great possibilities." Some historians, employing the term Taishō Democracy, associate the period with the emergence of political and social trends. Looking at a different set of trends, others have found it equally plausible to see in the Taishō period the roots of the radical nationalism, expansionism, and anti-liberalism that marked the 1930s and early 1940s.

THE CHANGE IN NATIONAL LEADERSHIP

The politics of compromise during the last decade of the Meiji period were interrupted by the Taishō Political Crisis of 1912–13, in which the third cabinet of Katsura Tarō was overthrown by the first Movement to Protect Constitutional Government.

For the next four years the *genrō* continued to nominate prestigious nonparty leaders to head the government. In reality, all cabinets found it necessary to rely on political party support in the Diet to carry on their programs, so that an embryonic two-party system was developing. Political influence shifted between the Seiyūkai and the Rikken Dōshikai (Constitutional Association of Friends; later reorganized as the Kenseikai, Constitutional Association). In 1918, Hara Takashi, president of the Seiyūkai, was recommended by the *genrō* as prime minister. For the next three years he presided over what can be seen as Japan's first party cabinet.

The assassination of Hara in 1921 temporarily halted the shift of national leadership to the political parties. The

ら1932年までは、再び政党のリーダーたちが首相を務めた。

第1次世界大戦と戦後の外交政策

第1次世界大戦の終戦を契機に、日本の外交政策は欧米の列強との協調政策に戻った。日本は1918年に、同盟国からシベリア出兵を要請されている。日本は列強の一員として、1919年のベルサイユ条約の交渉に参加し、新しく組織された国際連盟の常任理事国になった。

　1921年、アメリカの主唱によって、海軍軍縮問題を話し合い、東アジアの集団安全保障体制を議題とする、ワシントン会議が招集された。海軍軍縮条約は最終的に、イギリス、アメリカ、日本の主力艦の保有率を10：10：6にすることで合意に達している。

第1次世界大戦の影響

戦争の開始後、ヨーロッパの企業がアジアの市場から引き上げたことは、日本の工業の成長を促した。

　戦時景気は一獲千金による富をもたらした。1912年から1919年の間に、名目国民所得は3倍以上に膨らみ、42億円から133億円になったのである。

　好況はそれ以外にも社会的影響を及ぼした。工場労働者人口は2倍に膨らみ、とりわけ重工業に従事する男性労働者の比率が著しく高まった。当然ながら、労働争議の件数も増大し、1914年には50件しかなかった争議の記録が、1918年には417件になっている。しかしそれ以上に激しかったのは、1918年の米騒動である。米価の高騰

premiership, however, was held again by the leaders of major parties from 1924 until 1932.

WORLD WAR I AND POSTWAR FOREIGN POLICY

With the end of World War I, Japan returned to a policy of cooperation with the Western powers. In 1918, the allies requested that Japan contribute military forces to the Siberian Intervention. As one of the major powers, Japan participated in the negotiation of the Treaty of Versailles in 1919 and was given a seat on the council of the newly organized League of Nations.

In 1921, as the result of American initiative, the Washington Conference was convened to discuss the naval arms question and to devise collective security arrangements in East Asia. The naval treaty finally agreed upon a 10:10:6 ratio for the capital ship tonnage of the British, American, and Japanese fleets.

THE IMPACT OF WORLD WAR I

The withdrawal of European business interests from Asian markets after the war began provided a boost to the industrial sector.

The wartime boom brought with it a quick and easy prosperity. Between 1912 and 1919, the national income more than tripled in nominal terms, from ¥4.2 billion to ¥13.3 billion.

The boom had other social effects as well. The factory labor force nearly doubled in size, and the proportion of male workers in heavy industry rose significantly. Not surprisingly, the number of labor disputes increased. In 1914 there were only 50 recorded labor disputes, but in 1918 there were 417. More dramatic, however, were the rice riots of 1918. These massive popular demonstrations against exorbitant rice prices

に抗議する大規模な市民運動は、地方の農村
と小都市から、東京、大阪、京都などの大都市
へと広がった。路上にあふれた群衆は米屋や金
融業者などの店を襲い、略奪した。

戦後の不況

戦争が終わると同時に、好況も終わった。海外
市場の崩壊は1920年代に景気の後退をもたら
し、多くの企業が負債を抱え、新しい資金の調
達に苦しんだ。1923年の関東大震災は、日本の
重要な経済の中心京浜地方を広範囲にわたっ
て破壊した。その結果生じた1924年から25年の
「復興景気」は慢性的な不況の一時的な息抜き
になったが、昭和時代の初期には大恐慌が起こ
った（1927年の金融恐慌）。

民主主義の種子

1919年と1920年に、知識人、学生、それに労働
者が成年男子の普通選挙権を求めて、街頭でデ
モ行進をした。議会の野党は納税額による選挙
資格の廃止を支持したが、原敬内閣は1920年に
議会に提出された普通選挙法案を否決した。

　この結果に不満を抱いた都市の知識人と一
般市民の政治運動は1920年代の初期に過激化
した。1921年に結成された日本労働総同盟の
支配下の労働運動は、無政府主義の影響を受
けた労働組合至上主義（アナルコーサンジカリ
スム）、民主社会主義、あるいはマルクス主義に
傾倒した指導者の影響を受けた。学生団体もま
た過激化した。保守的な政治体制の最大の不
安を裏付けるように、1922年には日本共産党が
結成された。

spread from provincial villages and towns to major cities like Tōkyō, Ōsaka, and Kyōto. Crowds milled through the streets attacking and looting the shops of rice brokers, moneylenders, and other merchants.

THE POSTWAR DEPRESSION

When the war came to an end, so did the economic boom. The collapse of overseas markets brought about a recession in 1920. Many firms found themselves saddled with debt and unable to raise new capital. The Tōkyō Earhquake of 1923 caused widespread destruction in the Tōkyō-Yokohama area, one of the country's major economic centers. The "reconstruction boom" that resulted in 1924–25 provided a temporary respite from the chronic problems of the economy, but a major collapse occurred at the beginning of the Shōwa period (Financial Crisis of 1927).

THE SEEDS OF DEMOCRACY

In 1919 and 1920, intellectuals, students, and workers took to the streets to demonstrate for universal manhood suffrage. Although the opposition parties in the Diet favored an end to tax qualifications for voting, the party cabinet of Hara Takashi defeated a universal suffrage bill introduced into the 1920 Diet.

Frustrated by this failure, urban intellectuals and popular movements took a radical turn in the early 1920s. The labor movement, dominated by the Japan Federation of Labor (Sōdōmei), organized in 1921, and came under the influence of leaders committed to anarcho-syndicalism, democratic socialism, or Marxism. Student associations became radicalized as well. To confirm the worst fears of the conservative political establishment, the Japan Communist Party was organized in 1922.

議会は労働争議調停法、小作調停法、それに最低賃金法などの穏健な改革法案を成立させた。特筆すべきは、25歳以上の成人男子に選挙権を認めた、1925年の普通選挙法の成立である。1926年には、新しく選挙権を与えられた有権者を引きつけるために、労働農民党、日本労農党など、数多くの、小さな「プロレタリア政党」が結成された。

反動の種子

民主主義、改革、それに変革への趨勢の基盤は狭かった。日本の人口の大多数は、なおも因習と伝統的価値観が強く残る農村の共同社会で生活していた。

大学では、保守的な学生が過激派の影響力に対抗するために、自らを組織した。1924年には、国本社のような国家主義的思想団体が結成されている。

1925年の普通選挙法の成立が民主的傾向の兆候であったとすれば、同じ国会で成立した1925年の治安維持法は、それを相殺する保守的な、右翼的傾向を示していた。この法律は1926年に、大学生の急進的な活動を取り締まるために初めて適用された。1920年代の末には、特別高等警察(特高)が増強され、1930年代には、急進主義だけでなく、あらゆる種類の政治的反対意見を抑圧した。

文化

教育を受けた都市の中産階級は、西洋の書物の最新の翻訳を愛読し、文学、演劇、音楽、それに絵画の新しい実験の鑑賞者になった。新し

The Diet passed moderate reform legislation such as a labor exchange bill, a tenancy dispute arbitration law, and a minimum wage law. Most dramatically, in 1925 it passed a universal manhood suffrage law that gave the vote to adult males aged over twenty-five. To attract the newly enfranchised electorate, a number of small "proletarian parties" like the Labor-Farmer Party (Rōdō Nōmintō) and the Japan Labor-Farmer Party (Nihon Rōnōtō) were organized in 1926.

THE SEEDS OF REACTION

The trend toward democracy, reform, and change rested on a narrow base. The vast majority of the population still lived in rural communities where traditional folkways and values remained strong.

In the universities, conservative students organized themselves to counter the influence of student radicals. Nationalist organizations grew to include the Kokuhonsha (National Foundations Society), founded in 1924.

If the passage of the Universal Manhood Suffrage Law in 1925 marked the emergence of democratic trends, the Peace Preservation Law of 1925, passed by the same Diet, marked countervailing conservative and right-wing tendencies. In 1926, the law was invoked for the first time to crack down on student radicalism in the universities. In the late 1920s the forces of the Special Higher Police were expanded, and in the 1930s they were the principal instrument for controlling not only radicalism but all kinds of political dissent.

CULTURE

The educated urban middle classes avidly read the latest translations of Western books and provided the audience for new experiments in literature, drama, music, and painting.

いマスメディア（発行部数の多い新聞、『中央公
論』や『改造』などの月刊総合雑誌、それにラジ
オ放送）は文化生活の豊かさに貢献した。文学
上の重要な展開は、白樺派の出現である。武者
小路実篤、志賀直哉などのメンバーは、その上
流社会の生い立ちによって、また、その基本的
なヒューマニズムによって結ばれていた。洋画
では、安井曾太郎や梅原龍三郎がパリから戻っ
て、セザンヌやルノワールのスタイルを紹介した。
横山大観、菱田春草などの日本画家もまた、限
られた範囲内ではあるが、洋画の影響を受けた。

New kinds of mass media—large circulation newspapers, general monthly magazines like *Chūō kōron* (The Central Review) and *Kaizō*, and radio broadcasts—added to the richness of cultural life. The significant development in literature was the emergence of the Shirakaba school. Members of the group including Mushanokōji Saneatsu and Shiga Naoya were united by their upper-class background as well as by their basic humanism. In the Western-style of painting, Yasui Sōtarō and Umehara Ryūzaburō returned from Paris to promote the styles of Cézanne and Renoir. Japanese-style painters such as Yokoyama Taikan and Hishida Shunsō were also affected by European styles, although on a limited scale.

昭和時代

（1926〜89年）

1926年12月25日から1989年1月7日までの昭和天皇の治世は、歴代天皇のなかで最も長い治世で、とりわけ変動の激しい、論議をかもした時代だった。日本はこの62年間に、複雑な、しばしば矛盾する進路をたどり、議会制民主主義と平和的な国際協調の時代から、軍国主義と世界的な戦争の時代を、さらに敗戦と外国の軍隊による占領下の時代から復興と繁栄の時代を経験した。

Emperor Shōwa
(1901–89). When
Emperor Taishō died
in 1926, Hirohito
acceded to the throne
as Emperor Shōwa.
He was in ceremonial
robes worn for his
enthronement
ceremony in 1928.

議会政治と国際協力

昭和天皇が即位したとき、日本は西側諸国の民主主義の道を辿るかのように見えた。

しかし、大正時代の全体的に前向きの発展の陰には、重大な問題が潜んでいた。経済成長の恩恵に浴したのは、主として新興の財閥と都市部だった。小企業と農村人口の大部分は取り残され、深刻化する貧困に直面しなければならなかったのである。ついで、1927年の金融恐慌と、1929年のニューヨークの株式相場の大暴落が引き金になった昭和恐慌は、日本経済を混乱に陥れ、政府に寄せる一般市民の信頼を揺るがした。首相浜口雄幸が試みたデフレ政策と軍事ならびに行政予算の削減は、政治体制や政党政治に対する信頼の回復にはほとんど効果がなかった。政府はマルクス主義運動の激化を恐れ、共産主義の撲滅を口実に、1925年に成立させた治安維持法によって、反対意見を抑圧した。

Shōwa Period

(1926–89)

The reign of Emperor Shōwa (Hirohito), from 25 December 1926 to 7 January 1989, was the longest imperial reign in Japanese history, and one of the most tumultous and controversial. In the course of this sixty-two-year period, Japan traversed a complex and often contradictory course that led it from parliamentary democracy and peaceful international cooperation into militarism and global war, and then from defeat and occupation by foreign troops to recovery and a level of prosperity.

PARLIAMENTARIANISM AND INTERNATIONAL COOPERATION

When Emperor Shōwa ascended the throne, Japan appeared to be moving toward convergence with Western democracies.

Grave problems, however, were concealed in the background of the generally positive developments of the Taishō period. Economic growth seemed primarily to benefit the burgeoning financial conglomerates (*zaibatsu*) and the urban areas of the country; smaller businesses and the rural population were largely left behind to face increasingly difficult times. Then, in the Financial Crisis of 1927 and the Shōwa Depression touched off by the New York stock market crash of 1929, the Japanese economy was thrown into confusion, seriously shaking public confidence in the government. The deflationary policies and various military and bureaucratic budget cuts attempted by Prime Minister Hamaguchi Osachi did little to restore faith in the political system or in party rule. Fearful of a growing Marxist movement, government officials used the Peace Preservation Law of 1925 to suppress dissent in the name of eradicating communism.

軍国主義と権威主義

日本は徐々に1920年代の議会政治と国際協調主義から離れ、軍国主義と権威主義とアジアにおける「自主独往外交」政策へと移行した。1930年、浜口内閣がロンドン軍縮会議で、国際的な軍縮政策の続行に努めたことは、発言力を強めた軍部の大きな不満を買い、浜口自身は右翼に狙撃された。この状況は、1931年9月、攻撃的な陸軍将校が満州事変を工作し、1932年に傀儡国家の満州国を樹立すると、さらに悪化した。1933年、日本は国際連盟を脱退した。

それに追い討ちをかけるように、1936年、文民政治の基礎を揺るがす2・26事件が起こった。反乱は鎮圧されたが、政治の実権は次第に政党政治家の手を離れ、軍国主義者を抑制する能力を期待された人々に委ねられた。最初にこの新しいリーダーになったのは近衛文麿で、彼は1937年6月から1939年1月までと、さらに1940年7月から1941年10月まで首相を務めた。

近衛の人物像はなかなか捉えにくい。彼が抗争と混乱の終結を望んだことは疑いもないが、彼は気弱で、決断力に欠け、しかも、かなりの国粋主義者であったために、反動的な右派のスローガン「昭和維新」を抑えようとはしなかった。彼はそのうえ、1937年の盧溝橋事件が全面的な日中戦争に発展することを許した。日本は近衛の2度目の任期中に、イタリアとドイツとの運命の3国同盟（1940年）を締結した。この枢軸国に加わる決定は、1941年4月日ソ中立条約とともに、外相松岡洋右の考えを反映していた。断固とした態度と新しい同盟関係によって、アメリカとイギリ

MILITARISM AND AUTHORITARIANISM

Japan gradually moved away from the parliamentarianism and internationalism of the 1920s toward militarism, authoritarianism, and a "go-it-alone" policy in Asia. The Hamaguchi cabinet's efforts to continue a policy of international arms control at the London Naval Conference of 1930 were met with deep displeasure by an increasingly restive military, and Hamaguchi himself was shot by a right-wing assailant. The situation worsened in September 1931, when insubordinate army officers staged the Manchurian Incident, and then created the puppet state of Manchukuo in 1932. Japan withdrew from the League of Nations in 1933.

This was followed in 1936 by the shocking February 26th Incident that shook the very foundations of civilian government. The revolt was suppressed, but power increasingly slipped from the hands of party politicians into those of men who, it was hoped, might better be able to control the militarists. Foremost among these new leaders was Prince Konoe Fumimaro, who served as prime minister from June 1937 to January 1939, and again from July 1940 to October 1941.

Konoe was an ambiguous figure. Though he no doubt desired an end to conflict and chaos, he was weak and indecisive, and was enough of a nationalist that he did little to thwart those calling for a "Shōwa Restoration," the slogan of the reactionary right. Moreover, in 1937 he permitted the Marco Polo Bridge Incident to escalate into a full-scale war between China and Japan. During his second term of office, Konoe committed Japan to the fateful Tripartite Pact (1940) with Italy and Germany. This decision to join the Axis alliance, as well as the Soviet-Japanese Neutrality Pact signed in April 1941, reflected Foreign Minister Matsuoka Yōsuke's conviction that a firm stand and new allies would

スを牽制すれば、両国が第2次世界大戦初期の
ヨーロッパ戦線でのドイツ軍の圧倒的な勝利に
心を奪われていた当時の状況からみて、日本は
アジア太平洋地域を自由に支配できる、と彼は
確信したのである。

太平洋戦争

しかし、日本の行動はアメリカの機先を制するど
ころか、日米間の緊張を高めたに過ぎなかった。
アメリカは早くも1931年に、日本がこれ以上アジ
アを侵略することを認めないと宣言している。近
衛内閣は1941年10月に辞職し、東条英機陸軍
大将がその後継内閣を組織した。日米間の交
渉が、日本軍の中国からの撤兵問題で行き詰ま
った後、日本は1941年12月7日（日本時間で12
月8日）、真珠湾を攻撃し、東南アジアと太平洋
の大東亜共栄圏を、広範囲にわたって速やかに
占領した。

Zero Fighter
The range and
maneuver ability of
the Zero made it the
mainstay of Japan's
naval air forces and
one of the most
famous fighter planes
of World War II.

　初戦は日本が優勢だった。しかし、ミッドウェ
ー海戦やガダルカナル島での悽惨な戦いのころ
になると、日本にはそのように遠く離れた領土を
支配するための軍事力も、戦争の遂行を支える
物資や後方補給のための資源もないことが明ら
かになっていた。
　1945年には、日本の状況は絶望的だった。日
本はソ連の調停に期待をかけたが、アメリカ、イ
ギリス、それに中国が、1945年7月のポツダム宣
言のなかで明確に示した「無条件降伏」という厳
しい要求によって、その期待は粉砕された。日
本がためらう間に、原爆が広島と長崎に投下さ

persuade the United States and Great Britain to give Japan a free hand in Asia and the Pacific—especially given their preoccupation with the stunning German victories in the early phases of World War II in Europe.

PACIFIC WAR

Far from discouraging the United States, however, Japan's actions merely served to increase tensions. As early as 1931, the United States had said that it would not recognize further Japanese conquests in Asia. The Konoe cabinet resigned in October 1941, to be succeeded by a government formed by General Tōjō Hideki. After attempts at negotiation between Japan and the United States foundered over the issue of whether or not Japan should be permitted to maintain its military presence in China, Japan struck by surprise at Pearl Harbor on 7 December (8 December, Japanese time) 1941 and quickly occupied a vast area of Southeast Asia and the Pacific that it designated as the Greater East Asia Co-prosperity Sphere.

Initially the war went well for the Japanese. However, by the time of the Battle of Midway and the bloody campaign for Guadalcanal, it was clear that Japan did not have the forces necessary to control such far-flung territories, nor the material and logistic resources to sustain its war effort.

By 1945 Japan's situation was desperate. Japan turned to the USSR in the hope of finding an intermediary, but this hope was shattered by the firmly worded call for "unconditional surrender" enunciated by the United States, Great Britain, and China in the Potsdam Declaration of July 1945. As Japan hesitated, atomic bombs were dropped on Hiroshima

れ、ソ連が日本に宣戦を布告した。昭和天皇は、日本は「耐え難きを耐えなければならない」と判断し、敗北を認めた。1945年8月15日、第2次世界大戦は終結した。

占領

敗戦の結果、日本は連合国軍の占領下におかれ、この状態は1945年8月から1952年4月まで続いた。この間、日本の政府は連合国軍最高司令官（SCAP）の支配下におかれた。SCAPという言葉は最高司令官その人（1951年まではダグラス・マッカーサー将軍、その後はマッシュウ・B・リッジウェイ将軍）を指すと同時に、その占領政策の実施にあたる、大部分がアメリカ人の数千人からなる官僚機構を指す言葉として用いられた。占領体制の初期には、日本国憲法の制定、農地改革、教育改革、財閥の解体、また男女同権を支援し、日本の伝統的な家制度を廃止するために法律を大幅に改正するなど、広範囲に及ぶ一連の改革が断行された。

General Douglas MacArhur arrives at Atsugi Air Base near Tōkyō on 30 August 1945 to command the Allied Occupation of Japan.

　占領下で実施された、多くの突然の変革は、日本の保守的な人々に衝撃を与えた。彼らをとりわけ憤慨させたのは、天皇の地位が憲法によって、純粋に象徴的なものにされたこと、憲法第9条に示される軍備の放棄、警察ならび教育制度の地方分権化、それに、多くの戦前の政界ならびに財界の指導者の公職追放である。しかし同時に日本の左翼活動家や進歩主義者もまた、より徹底した社会構造の改革が行われなかったことに失望し、占領の後期には、冷戦の緊張を反映した占領政策の「逆行」に落胆した。1950

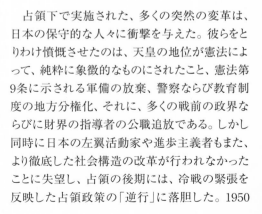

and Nagasaki, and the Soviet Union declared war on Japan. Emperor Shōwa decided that Japan would have to "bear the unbearable" and accept its defeat. On 15 August 1945, World War II came to an end.

OCCUPATION

As a result of its defeat, Japan was subjected to the Allied Occupation, which lasted from August 1945 to April 1952. During this period the Japanese government was subject to the authority of the Supreme Commander for the Allied Powers (SCAP), a term that referred both to the commander himself (General Douglas MacArthur until 1951 and then General Matthew B. Ridgway) and to the supporting bureaucracy of several thousand officials, most of them Americans. During the early years of the Occupation, they pushed through a sweeping series of reforms that included the Constitution of Japan, the Land Reforms of 1946, a revamping of the educational system, curtailment of the economic activities of the *zaibatsu*, and major changes in the legal codes to support equality of the sexes and lessen the authority of Japan's traditional patriarchal family system.

The many sudden changes instituted under the Occupation shocked Japan's conservatives. Particularly galling were the constitution's reduction of the emperor to purely symbolic status, the renunciation of a military establishment contained in Article 9, the decentralization of the police and educational system, and the banning from public life of thousands of pre-war political and business leaders (Occupation Purge). At the same time, Japanese leftists and progressives were disappointed that even more fundamental structural reforms had not been carried out, and in the later years of the Occupation they were dismayed by what they saw as a

年の朝鮮戦争の勃発後には、警察予備隊（やが
て現在の自衛隊に発展した）が設置されている。

　占領体制は1951年9月に日本と非共産圏の48
か国の間にサンフランシスコ平和条約が締結さ
れて、1952年4月、正式に終わった。日本はそ
れと同時に日米安全保障条約を締結した。

繁栄への道

日本経済はなおも苦しい戦後の復興過程にあっ
たが、アメリカの支援、1ドルが360円という安定
した為替相場、朝鮮戦争によるアメリカ軍と国連
軍の支援のための特別軍事需要（特需）、それ
に日本の実業界と労働者階級の努力が結びつ
いて、日本の国民総生産（GNP）の平均伸び率
を1951年から55年には8.6パーセント、1955年か
ら60年には9.1パーセント以上に押しあげた。

　政治面には多少の動揺があった。与党自由
民主党による憲法第9条を含む、いくつかの占領
政策の変更、あるいは後戻り修正の試みには、
日本社会党や日本共産党が激しく反対した。そ
の緊張は1960年6月、岸信介首相が在日米軍基
地問題に決着を付けようと、日米安保条約を改
正し、その国会批准を強行したときに極度の興
奮状態に達した。新安保条約は空前の規模の
反対闘争の末に成立したが、その混乱によって
ドワイト・D・アイゼンハワー大統領の日本訪問
は中止され、岸は辞任に追い込まれた。新首相
池田勇人（1960〜64年）とその後継者佐藤栄作
（1964〜72年）はそれ以降、「所得倍増」という高

"reverse course" in Occupation policy, reflecting Cold War tensions. After the outbreak of the Korean War in 1950, the National Police Reserve (which later evolved into the present Self-Defense Forces) was created.

The Occupation officially ended in April 1952 with the implementation of the San Francisco Peace Treaty, which Japan had signed with 48 noncommunist nations in September 1951. At the same time, Japan concluded a security treaty with the United States.

TOWARD PROSPERITY

Japan's economy was still in the arduous process of recovery from the war, but U.S. aid, a stable ¥360-to-$1.00 exchange rate, a rush of special military procurements (*tokuju*) to support the U.S. and United Nations forces in the Korean War, and hard work by Japanese business and labor combined to push the average annual growth of Japan's gross national product (GNP) to 8.6 percent in 1951–55, and over 9.1 percent in 1955–60.

The political scene was more turbulent. Attempts by the ruling Liberal Democratic Party (LDP) to alter or roll back a number of the Occupation reforms, including Article 9 of the constitution, were met with fierce protests by the Japan Socialist Party (JSP) and the Japan Communist Party (JCP). Tension reached a fever pitch in June 1960, when Prime Minister Kishi Nobusuke rammed a revised United States–Japan Security Treaty through the Diet in the hope of resolving controversy over the U.S. bases in Japan. After massive rioting, the revised treaty went into effect, but the turmoil forced President Dwight D. Eisenhower to cancel his visit and Kishi to resign. The new prime minister, Ikeda Hayato (1960–64), and his successor, Satō Eisaku (1964–72), now concentrated on an "income-doubling" policy of high economic growth.

度経済成長政策に努力を集中した。

急速な経済成長は昭和時代の最後の20年間
の支配的なテーマになった。1970年代の初期に
は、日本は船舶、ラジオ、それにテレビの世界一
の生産国になった。そして1980年代には、自動
車の製造で世界をリードし、また、ビデオ・カセッ
トテープ、集積回路、ビデオゲームなど、ハイテ
ク製品の主要な生産国になっている。海外から
の輸出自主規制の圧力にもかかわらず、また、円
とドルの為替比率の不均衡を是正しようとする懸
命の努力にもかかわらず、日本の貿易収支はと
りわけアメリカに対して、大幅な黒字が続いた。

この時代の日本の高度成長にはいくつかの理
由があった。その第1は、日本の人口が1945年
の7,200万人から、1989年には1億2,000万人に増
加し、日本が世界で第7位の人口を擁する大国
になったことである。第2は、日本の低比率の防
衛費（通常GNPの1パーセント以下）、比較的低
比率の社会保障費用、それに全体的に高い貯蓄
率が、最新技術と革新的なプラントや設備への
大口の資本投資を可能にしたことである。日本
の実業界は教育水準の高い、勤勉な労働力人
口を活用して、優れた製品の量産を実現した。

昭和時代末期の日本の社会

日本の急速な工業化は、1980年代までに、日本
の人口の80パーセントを都市に集中させ、家族
制度も伝統的な大家族から現代的な核家族へ
と移行した。強い信仰をもつ家庭は少なかった
が、従来の宗教である仏教と神道は繁栄した。
犯罪と麻薬は、ほかの先進工業国に比べて、驚
くほど低レベルに留まった。

Rapid economic growth provided the dominant theme of the last twenty years of Emperor Shōwa's reign. By the early 1970s, Japan was the world's largest producer of ships, radios, and televisions. By the 1980s, Japan had become the leading manufacturer of cars in the world, and the dominant producer of such high-technology electronic products as videocassette recorders, computer chips, and video games. Despite pressures from abroad for voluntary restraints on exports, and vigorous efforts to correct the imbalance in the yen-dollar exchange rate, Japan's favorable trade balances, especially with the United States, remained large.

There were many reasons for Japan's high rate of growth during this period. First, Japan's demographic growth from a population of 72 million in 1945 to more than 120 million in 1989 made it the seventh most populous nation in the world. Second, Japan's low military expenditures (usually below 1 percent of GNP), relatively low investment in social services, and generally high rate of savings contributed to heavy capital investment in the latest technology and innovative plants and equipment. The Japanese business community made use of a well-educated and hardworking labor force to turn out a stream of highly successful products.

JAPANESE SOCIETY AT THE END OF THE SHŌWA PERIOD

By the 1980s, Japan's rapid industrialization had brought more than 80 percent of the Japanese population into urban areas, and there was a shift from the traditional extended-family ideal to the more modern nuclear family. Few families professed to be very religious, yet the established Buddhist and Shintō sects prospered. The level of crime and the proliferation of illegal drugs remained surprisingly low in comparison to other advanced industrial nations.

とはいえ、日本の社会は困難な問題も抱えていた。1970年代の初期には、公害病で衝撃を受けた国民に、高度成長の環境に及ぼす悪影響が認識された。1973年の石油危機と、1970年代のアメリカの大統領リチャード・M・ニクソンによる一連の一方的な行動（ニクソン・ショック）もまた、日本の貿易黒字に対する諸外国の抗議が高まるなかで、外国の事情や外国からの圧力によって傷つきやすい日本経済の体質を強く自覚させた。政府は財政赤字削減のために、歳出の引き締め、国鉄などの政府事業の民営化を進めた。また、日本の人口の急速な高齢化に備えて、社会保障の改善のための資金調達を主な目的として、1988年に3パーセントの消費税を導入した。

1970年代に始まった一連の政治的なスキャンダルもまた、日本の政党政治の性格が引き続き批判されるきっかけになった。首相田中角栄（1972〜74年）は、当初国内問題への精力的な取り組みを称えられたが、まもなくロッキード事件に巻き込まれ、辞任に追い込まれた。国民の不満は1988年の消費税の成立後、またしても高まった。消費税そのものに問題があったばかりでなく、たまたま、その成立と同時期に、リクルート社が多くの指導的な政治家を不法な株式取り引きに関与させた事実が明らかにされたからである（リクルート事件）。与党の自民党はこの間ずっと政権を維持し続けた。その理由は主として、野党の日本社会党、日本共産党、それに公明党などがあまりにも無力で、しかも互いに対立していたために、効果的な連立政権を形成できなかったことにあるが、それだけではなく、自民党自

The literary giants Mishima Yukio and Kawabata Yasunari committed suicide, radical students fought bitter battles over New Tōkyō International Airport, and other intellectuals such as Ōe Kenzaburō spoke bitterly of present-day absurdities; many people wondered if the best years of the post-war period had passed.

The Shōwa period thus drew to a close on a rather ambiguous note.

平成時代

（1989～　）

現在の天皇の治世で、1989年1月7日、昭和
天皇の崩御に伴い、皇太子明仁親王が
皇位を継承した。平成という年号は中国の古典、
『史記』と『書経』からの2つの引用に基づいて定
められ、天上と地上での、また国内と海外での
平和の達成を意味している。1979年の元号法に
よって定められた、最初の元号である。

政治

自民党政治の腐敗に対する一般市民の憤りは
続いた。

　自民党は衆議院議員選挙に比例代表制度と
小選挙区制度を導入するなどの政治改革を真
剣に検討し始めた。

　自民党による政治改革の遅れは、1993年、離
党者による新生党と新党さきがけの結成へと事
態を展開させた。1993年の選挙はかつてない
自民党の敗北と、社会党の予想外の後退に終
わった。この2大政党の選挙戦での惨敗は、
1955年体制に終止符を打った。1993年8月、細
川護熙を首相とする連立内閣が組織され、1994
年1月、彼のもとでようやく政治改革法案が一括
して承認された。

　細川政権は1994年4月、細川の辞任によって、
わずか8か月で終わった。後継首相には、同じ
連立与党によって羽田孜（つとむ）が選ばれた。しかし、

Heisei Period

(1989–   )

The reign of the present emperor, Akihito, who ascended the throne at the death of his father, Emperor Shōwa, on 7 January 1989. The era name Heisei is based on two quotations from the Chinese classics *Shi ji* (Book of History) and *Shu jing* (Book of Documents) that signify the attainment of peace in heaven and on earth, at home and abroad. It is the first era name to be selected and given official recognition under the Gengō Law of 1979.

POLITICS

Public anger over political corruption in the Liberal Democratic Party (LDP) has continued.

The LDP began serious deliberations over reform measures that would introduce proportional representation and smaller election districts into elections for the House of Representatives.

The LDP's repeated failure to carry out political reforms led to the breakaway of dissidents who formed the Shinseitō (New Life Party) and Shintō Sakigake (Harbinger Party) parties in 1993. The 1993 election resulted in an unprecedented defeat for the LDP and an equally unexpected setback for the JSP. The electoral defeats suffered by these two political parties marked the end of the 1955 status quo. A coalition government was formed in August 1993 under Prime Minister Hosokawa Morihiro who finally succeeded in passing a political reform package in January 1994.

The Hosokawa government lasted only eight months with Hosokawa resigning in April 1994. Selected by the same group of coalition parties, Hata Tsutomu replaced Hosokawa.

ほとんどその直後に、社会党と新党さきがけが連立政権を離れ、自民党がすぐさま、社会党と新党さきがけと共に、社会党の村山富市を首相とする連立内閣を組織した。

1994年12月、6つの政党・団体が集まって、新進党を結成した。

経済

日本のいわゆる「バブル経済」は1986年に始まり、1991年5月に初めて後退の兆候を見せた。1993年には、東京の地価は1990年の投機的な頂点の50パーセント下落し、1993年の日経平均株価指数の終値も、1989年末の記録の半分以下になっていた。

1993年春には、2、3の景気回復の兆しが現れたが、これらは一時的で、経済の全域には広がらず、景気の沈滞は続いた。1993年の夏から著しい円高が始まり、1995年3月には1ドルが90円を割った。円の高騰は日本の経済に大きな打撃を与えた。すでに低迷していた製造業はまもなく大規模なリストラを余儀なくされ、多くの企業が前例のない人員整理に踏み切った。大手の製造業者がつぎつぎに生産拠点を海外に移すなかで、産業の空洞化が懸念されている。

また、金融機関はいまもなお、バブル経済時代に抱え込んだ不良債権の重荷に苦しんでおり、景気回復の足どりは重い。

Almost immediately, however the JSP and Shintō Sakigake left the coalition. The LDP immediately joined with the JSP and Shintō Sakigake to form a coalition government, with JSP member Murayama Tomiichi as prime minister.

In December 1994, six parties and groups joined together to form the Shinshintō (New Frontier Party).

ECONOMY

Japan's so-called "bubble economy" began in 1986 and first started to show signs of receding in May 1991. By 1993, the price of land in Tōkyō had fallen 50 percent from its 1990 speculative peak, and the average closing price of the Nikkei stock market index in 1993 was less than half that recorded at the end of 1989.

Isolated signs of recovery were evident in the spring of 1993, but these were short-lived and did not extend to the economy as a whole, which remained sluggish. The yen showed a marked increase in strength beginning in the summer of 1993, even exceeding ¥90 per U.S. dollar in March 1995. The rise of the yen was a strong blow to the Japanese economy: industry, already stagnant at the time, was soon forced to undertake large-scale restructuring; many companies even made unprecedented adjustments to their personnel structures. Observers warned of a possible hollowing-out of industry, as one major manufacturer after another moves its manufacturing operations overseas. Finally, financial institutions continued to labor under a heavy burden of bad debts taken on during the bubble economy.

It will likely be some time before the economy shows any real improvement.

社会

1995年8月15日、日本は第2次世界大戦の終戦
50周年を迎えた。戦後の日本の発展に関する
さまざまな世論調査で、多くの市民は日本の経
済成長、生活水準の向上、それに平和の維持
に、満足の意を表明している。

　その一方で、日本の社会は出生率の低下や
人口の急速な高齢化など、新しい問題に取り組
み始めた。

　1995年1月、淡路島の北端を震源地とするマ
グニチュード7.2の大地震が、神戸をはじめ阪神
地方を広範囲にわたって破壊し、6,308人の死者
と32万人の被災者を出した。これは、日本で戦
後最大の大惨事となった（阪神大震災）。1995年
3月には、致命的な神経ガス、サリンが新興宗教
オウム真理教の信徒によって、東京の地下鉄で
撒かれた。関西の地震の破壊力に動揺してい
た一般市民は、カルト組織による社会全体への
無差別攻撃を初めて経験して、大きな衝撃を受
けた。

　日本は徐々に、しかし着実に、社会を多様化
し、その経済力に見合う国際的な責任を負うこ
とに努めている。日本のODA（政府開発援助）
は1994年、132億USドルに達した。1992年、国
会は国連平和維持活動（PKO）協力法を承認し、
1992年10月、自衛隊がカンボジアに派遣された。

SOCIETY

Japan observed the fiftieth anniversary of the end of World War II on August 15, 1995. In various public opinion polls on Japan's postwar achievements, citizens still express their overall satisfaction with the country's economic growth, high standard of living, and successful maintenance of peace.

On the other hand, society has recently begun to grapple with such new problems as a lower birth rate and a rapidly aging population.

In January 1995, the Kōbe Earthquake (Great Hanshin Earthquake)—with its magnitude of 7.2 and epicenter in the northern tip of the island of Awajishima—destroyed much of the Hanshin area, particularly Kōbe, leaving a total of 6,308 dead and 320,000 injured. This was the largest natural disaster in Japan's post-war history. In March 1995, the deadly nerve gas sarin was released into Tōkyō's subways in an attack perpetrated by members of the new religion Aum Shinrikyō. Japan's first experience of an attack against society-at-large by a cult organization sent deep shock waves through a public already reeling from the destructiveness of the quake in Kansai.

Japan has continued its slow but steady efforts to achieve greater diversity in its social fabric and shoulder international responsibility consistent with its economic power. Japan's ODA reached US$13.2 billion in 1994. In 1992, the Diet enacted the Law on Cooperation in United Nations Peace Keeping Operations (PKO), and Japanese Self Defense Forces were sent to Cambodia in October of that year.

日本史年表

Chronology of
Japanese History

168 日本の
　　　歴史

Japanese History

Prehistory
(Before ca. A.D. 300)

Before 30,000 B.C.	Paleolithic culture.
Ca. 10,000 B.C.	Jōmon culture.
Ca. 300 B.C.	Yayoi culture emerges with the introduction of wet-rice cultivation.
Ca. A.D. 1	Japan mentioned in Chinese historical records as the land of Wa, composed of a number of states.
57	King of the state of Na in Wa offers tribute to the Later Han dynasty and is awarded a gold seal.
239	Himiko sends an envoy to the kingdom of Wei.

Kofun period
(ca. 300–710)

350	The Yamato Court established by this time.
552	Traditional date for introduction of Buddhism to Japan. An earlier date, 538, is assigned by many scholars.
587	Soga no Umako kills Mononobe no Moriya.
593	Prince Shōtoku appointed regent.
604	Seventeen Article Constitution is promulgated.
607	Ono no Imoko appointed leader of the second embassy of Sui China.
630	First embassy to Tang-dynasty China dispatched.

World History

Prehistory

旧石器文化	
縄文文化	
弥生文化、水稲農業始まる	334 B.C. Alexander the Great begins his conquest of the East. アレクサンダー大王の東征始まる
倭、小国分立	
	221 B.C. China unified under the Qin dynasty (221 B.C.–206 B.C.). 秦朝、中国統一
倭の奴国王、後漢に入貢、印綬をうける	
卑弥呼、魏に遣使	
この頃大和朝廷成立	
	476 Romulus Augustulus, the last emperor of the Western Roman Empire, deposed by the Goths under Odoacer. オドアケル、西ローマ帝国最後の皇帝アウグストルスを廃位
仏教伝来 (一説に538年)	
蘇我馬子、物部守屋を滅ぼす	589 Beginning of the Sui dynasty (589–618) in China. 中国に隋朝成立
聖徳太子、摂政となる	
十七条憲法制定	
小野妹子を隋に派遣	622 Prophet Muhammad arrives in Medina; the Islamic Era begins. マホメッド、メデイナに到着；イスラム暦元年
	624 China unified under the Tang dynasty (618–907). 中国に唐朝成立
第1回遣唐使	

645	Taika Reform initiated.
701	Taihō Code completed.

Nara period (710–794)

710	Heijōkyō established.
712	Compilation of the *Kojiki* (Record of Ancient Matters) is completed by Ō no Yasumaro.
720	*Nihon shoki* (Chronicle of Japan) completed.
723	Law of Three Generations or a Lifetime put into effect.
733	Regional gazetteer *Izumo fudoki* completed.
743	Konden Einen Shizai Hō promulgated.
752	The Great Buddha at Tōdaiji is completed.
759	The *Man'yōshū* (Collection of Ten Thousand Leaves) completed around this time.
784	Capital moved to Nagaokakyō.
788	Saichō, founder of the Tendai sect, establishes the temple of Enryakuji.

Heian period (794–1185)

794	Capital moved to Heiankyō.
823	Kūkai, founder of the Shingon sect, appointed abbot of Tōji.
866	Fujiwara no Yoshifusa establishes himself as regent.
905	The *Kokin wakashū* (Collection from Ancient and Modern Times) is completed.
935	Ki no Tsurayuki composes the *Tosa nikki* (*The Tosa Diary*), written in the native *kana* syllabary.
	Rebellion by Taira no Masakado (935–940).
996	Sei Shōnagon's *Makura no sōshi* (*The Pillow Book*) is now in circulation.

大化の改新	
大宝律令	668 Silla unifies Korea with the assistance of Tang China. 新羅、朝鮮統一
平城京遷都	
太安万侶「古事記」撰上	
「日本書紀」	
三世一身の法	
「出雲風土記」	
墾田永年私財法	
東大寺大仏開眼供養会	
「万葉集」この頃に完成	
長岡京遷都	
天台宗開祖最澄、延暦寺を造る	
平安京に遷都	800 Charlemagne crowned by Pope Leo III as Charles I, emperor of the Holy Roman Empire. カール大帝、教皇によりローマ皇帝として戴冠される
真言宗開祖空海、東寺を与えられる	
藤原良房、摂政となる	
「古今和歌集」	
紀貫之、仮名文字で「土佐日記」を書く	
平将門の乱	960 Beginning of the Northern Song dynasty (960–1126) in China. 中国に北宋おこる
清少納言「枕草子」	

1008	Murasaki Shikibu's *Tale of Genji* has now been written.
1016	Fujiwara no Michinaga becomes regent.
1053	Construction of the Phoenix Hall completed at the temple of Byōdōin.
1069	Emperor Go-Sanjō establishes the Office for the Investigation of Shōen Documents.
1087	Emperor Shirakawa abdicates, establishes the system of "cloister government."
1156	Hōgen Disturbance.
1160	Heiji Disturbance.
1167	Taira no Kiyomori is made grand minister of state.
1180	Taira-Minamoto War begins.
Kamakura period (1185–1333)	
1185	Minamoto no Yoshitsune annihilates the Taira family in the Battle of Dannoura.
	Minamoto no Yoritomo receives from the imperial court the right to appoint provincial constables and estate stewards.
1191	Eisai, founder of the Rinzai sect, returns from China and begins to advocate Chinese Zen teaching.
1192	Minamoto no Yoritomo assumes the title of *seii tai shōgun* (Barbarian-subduing Generalissimo).
1203	Hōjō Tokimasa assumes the office of shogunal regent.
	Kaikei and Unkei sculpt the pair of guardian deities housed in the Great South Gate at the temple of Tōdaiji.
1205	*Shin kokin wakashū* (New Collection from Ancient and Modern Times) is submitted to the throne by Fujiwara no Sadaie and others.
1212	Kamo no Chōmei completes his essay *Hōjōki* (*An Account of My Hut*).

紫式部「源氏物語」

藤原道長、摂政となる

平等院鳳凰堂完成

後三条天皇、記録荘園券
契所を設置

白河上皇の院政始まる

保元の乱

平治の乱

平清盛、太政大臣となる

源平の争乱

源義経、壇ノ浦の戦いで
平氏一門を滅す

源頼朝の奏請で守護、地
頭設置

栄西帰国し、臨済宗を広
める

頼朝、征夷大将軍となる

北条時政、執権になる

快慶、運慶、東大寺南大
門の金剛力士像を完成

藤原定家「新古今和歌集」
撰進

鴨長明「方丈記」

1066 William, duke of Normandy, is
crowned king of England.
ノルマン朝、イギリス征服

1096 The first expedition of the
Crusaders.
十字軍始まる

1127 Beginning of the Southern Song
dynasty (1127–1279) in China.
中国に南宋おこる

1218	Early versions of the *Heike monogatari* (*The Tale of the Heike*) in existence by about this time.
1221	Jōkyū Disturbance.
1224	Shinran completes the *Kyōgyōshinshō* (A Collection of Passages Revealing the True Teaching, Practice, and Attainment of the Pure Land); Jōdo Shin sect is established.
1227	Dōgen establishes the Sōtō sect.
1232	Goseibai Shikimoku (The Formulary of Adjudications) promulgated.
1253	Nichiren establishes the Nichiren sect.
1274	First of the Mongol invasions of Japan.
1279	Ippen, the founder of the Ji sect, starts preaching the "dancing *nembutsu*."
1281	Second of the Mongol invasions of Japan.
1330	Yoshida Kenkō completes the collection of essays *Tsurezuregusa* (*Essays in Idleness*).

Muromachi period (1333–1568)

1333	Kamakura shogunate collapses.
	Kemmu Restoration (1333–1336).
1337	Emperor Go-Daigo escapes to Yoshino and establishes the Southern Court.
1338	Ashikaga Takauji receives the title of *seii tai shōgun*, founds the Muromachi shogunate.
1370	From around this time fleets of Japanese pirates pillage coastal areas of China and Korea.
1392	Northern and Southern Courts reconciled.
1397	Ashikaga Yoshimitsu begins construction of Kitayama-dono (later becomes Kinkakuji; Temple of the Golden Pavilion).

「平家物語」

承久の乱
親鸞「教行信証」成る、浄土真宗開宗

道元、曹洞宗を開く
御成敗式目制定

日蓮、日蓮宗を開く
文永の役（第1回蒙古襲来）
時宗開祖一遍、踊念仏を始める
弘安の役（第2回蒙古襲来）
吉田兼行「徒然草」

鎌倉幕府滅亡
建武の中興
後醍醐天皇、南朝を開く

足利尊氏、征夷大将軍となる
倭寇の活動さかん

南北朝合一
足利義満、北山殿（金閣寺）を造営

1215 Magna Carta issued, under duress, by King John of England.
マグナ・カルタ発布

1271 Marco Polo sets out on his journey to the court of the Mongol emperor Kublai Khan.
マルコ・ポーロ、東方旅行に出発

1279 Kublai Khan conquers the Southern Song and establishes the Yuan dynasty (1279–1368) in China.
クビライ・ハン、南宋征服、元朝中国統一

1337 Hundred Years' War begins.
英仏百年戦争始まる

1347 Black Death rages in Europe (1347–51).
ヨーロッパにペスト流行

1368 Zhu Yuanzhang founds the Ming dynasty (1368–1644) in China.
朱元璋、中国に明朝をおこす

1392 Yi Sŏng-gye founds the Yi dynasty (1392–1910) in Korea.
李成桂、李氏朝鮮建国

1400	Zeami completes the first three chapters of the *Fūshi kaden* (Transmission of the Flower of Acting Style).
1404	Tally trade initiated with Ming-dynasty China.
1428	Peasant uprising in Kyōto and surrounding provinces.
1467	Ōnin War begins (1467–77).
1483	Ashikaga Yoshimasa settles at the villa that later becomes Ginkakuji (Temple of the Silver Pavillion); this becomes known as the center of Higashiyama culture.
1488	Adherents of the Jōdo Shin sect establish autonomous rule in Kaga Province (Ikkō *ikki*: Single-minded Uprising).
1495	Sesshū Tōyō produces *Haboku sansuizu* (Haboku Landscape).
1543	Matchlock muskets are introduced to Japan by the Portuguese on Tanegashima.
1549	Francis Xavier establishes Japan's first Christian mission at Kagoshima.
Azuchi-Momoyama period (1568–1600)	
1568	Oda Nobunaga enters Kyōto.
1573	Oda Nobunaga ousts Ashikaga Yoshiaki; Muromachi shogunate collapses.
1582	Honnōji Incident; Oda Nobunaga is assassinated by Akechi Mitsuhide.
	Toyotomi Hideyoshi initiates the Taikō *kenchi* (cadastral surveys by Taikō).
1588	Toyotomi Hideyoshi issues the order of sword hunt.
1590	Toyotomi Hideyoshi pacifies all of Japan.
1591	Sen no Rikyū is forced to commit suicide by Hideyoshi.

世阿弥「風姿花伝」

明との勘合貿易始まる

京畿で土一揆

応仁の乱

足利義政、銀閣を造営；
東山文化の中心となる

加賀の一向一揆、一国を
支配

雪舟等楊「破墨山水図」

ポルトガル人、種子島に
鉄砲を伝える

ザビエル、キリスト教を伝
える

織田信長、入京

室町幕府滅亡

本能寺の変

太閤検地開始

刀狩令

豊臣秀吉、全国統一

千利休自刃

1455 Johannes Gutenberg completes the Forty-Two Line Bible, printed from movable type.
グーテンベルク、聖書を活字印刷

1492 Christopher Columbus lands in the Bahamas.
コロンブス、バハマ諸島に上陸

1498 Vasco da Gama, after a voyage around the Cape of Good Hope, reaches Calicut in India.
バスコ・ダ・ガマ、インドのカリカットに到着

1517 Martin Luther nails the Ninety-Five Theses to the church door at Wittenberg.
ルター「95箇条の論題」；宗教改革を始める

1592	First of the invasions of Korea.
1597	Second of the invasions of Korea.
Edo period (1600–1868)	
1600	Battle of Sekigahara
1603	Tokugawa Ieyasu is granted the title of *seii tai shōgun*, founds the Tokugawa shogunate.
1612	Shogunate issues directives aimed at restricting Christianity (anti-Christian edicts).
1614	The Winter's Siege of Ōsaka Castle.
1615	The Summer Campaign of Ōsaka Castle; Toyotomi Hideyori commits suicide.
	Shogunate promulgates the Buke Shohatto (Laws for the Military Houses) and Kinchū Narabi ni Kuge Shohatto (Laws Governing the Imperial Court and Nobility).
1635	System of mandatory alternate residence in Edo by *daimyō* formalized.
1636	Dejima at Nagasaki completed.
1637	Shimabara Uprising (1637–38).
1639	Edicts establishing National Seclusion are completed.
1682	Ihara Saikaku publishes *Kōshoku ichidai otoko* (*The Life of an Amorous Man*).
1688	Beginning of the Genroku era (1688–1704); the golden age of *kabuki* and *jōruri*.
1689	Matsuo Bashō departs on the journey of *Oku no hosomichi* (*The Narrow Road to the Deep North*).
1703	Band of former retainers of the Akō domain, under the leadership of Ōishi Yoshio, carry out a vendetta against Kira Yoshinaka (Forty-Seven Rōnin Incident).
	First performance of *Sonezaki shinjū* (*The Love Suicide at Sonezaki*), written by Chikamatsu Monzaemon.

文禄の役

慶長の役

関ケ原の戦い

徳川家康、征夷大将軍となり徳川幕府を開く

禁教令

大坂冬の陣

大坂夏の陣、豊臣氏滅亡

武家諸法度および禁中並公家諸法度発布

参勤交代制を定める

長崎出島成る

島原の乱

鎖国が完成する

井原西鶴「好色一代男」

元禄時代始まる；歌舞伎、浄瑠璃が隆盛になる

松尾芭蕉「奥の細道」の旅に出立

赤穂浪士大石良雄ら、吉良義央を討つ

近松門左衛門「曽根崎心中」初演

1600 British East India Company incorporated by royal charter.
イギリス東インド会社設立

1602 Dutch establish the Dutch East India Company.
オランダ東インド会社設立

1644 Manchus establish the Qing dynasty (1644–1912) in China.
中国、清朝成立

1689 English Bill of Rights enacted.
英国権利宣言公布

1709	Arai Hakuseki becomes a key shogunal adviser.
1716	Tokugawa Yoshimune becomes *shōgun*; Kyōhō Reforms (1716–45) commence.
1721	*Meyasubako* is posted.
1767	Tanuma Okitsugu becomes grand chamberlain.
1774	*Kaitai shinsho* (New Book of Anatomy) published by Sugita Gempaku and Maeno Ryōtaku.
1776	Ueda Akinari publishes *Ugetsu monogatari* (*Tales of Moonlight and Rain*).
1782	Temmei Famine (1782–87) begins.
1787	Matsudaira Sadanobu becomes senior shogunal councillor; Kansei Reforms (1787–93) initiated.
1798	Motoori Norinaga completes the *Kojiki den*, a major work in the National Learning movement.
1800	Inō Tadataka begins his cartographic survey of all Japan (1800–16).
1802	Jippensha Ikku publishes the first volume of *Tōkaidōchū hizakurige* (*Shank's Mare*).
1807	Takizawa Bakin begins publication of *Chinsetsu yumiharizuki* (Crescent Moon: The Adventures of Tametomo).
1809	Mamiya Rinzō discovers the Tatar Strait.
1820	Kobayashi Issa completes *Oraga haru* (*The Year of My Life*).
1825	Shogunate issues the Gaikokusen Uchiharai Rei (Order for the Repelling of Foreign Ships).
1831	Katsushika Hokusai's series of *ukiyo-e Fugaku sanjūrokkei* (Thirty-Six Views of Mt. Fuji) begins to appear by about this time.
1833	Tempō Famine (1833–36) begins.
	Publication of Andō Hiroshige's *ukiyo-e Tōkaidō gojūsantsugi* (Fifty-Three Stations of the Tōkaidō Road) begins.

幕府、新井白石を登用

徳川吉宗将軍になる；享保の改革

目安箱設置

田沼意次、側用人となる

杉田玄白、前野良沢「解体新書」

上田秋成「雨月物語」

天明の飢饉

松平定信、老中となる；寛政の改革

本居宣長「古事記伝」

伊能忠敬、地図測量始める

十返舎一九「東海道中膝栗毛」

滝沢馬琴「椿説弓張月」

間宮林蔵、タタール海峡（間宮海峡）を発見

小林一茶「おらが春」

外国船打払令

葛飾北斎「富嶽三十六景」

天保の飢饉

安藤広重「東海道五十三次」

1776 Continental Congress issues the U.S. Declaration of Independence.
アメリカ独立宣言公布

1789 French Revolution begins.
フランス革命始まる

1804 Napoleon crowns himself emperor of France.
ナポレオン、皇帝となる

1837	Rebellion of Ōshio Heihachirō.
1839	Bansha no Goku (Imprisonment of the Companions of Barbarian Studies).
1841	Tempō Reforms (1841–43) initiated by Mizuno Tadakuni.
1853	Four warships of the U.S. East India Squadron, commanded by Commodore Matthew Perry, call at Uraga.
1854	Kanagawa Treaty (Treaty of Peace and Amity between the United States and the Empire of Japan) signed.
1858	Ansei commercial treaties are concluded.
	Beginning of the Ansei Purge (1858–60).
1860	Assassination of Ii Naosuke (Sakuradamongai Incident).
1866	Satsuma-Chōshū Alliance formed against the Tokugawa shogunate.
	The second of the Chōshū Expeditions.
1867	Formal return of political authority to the emperor by Tokugawa Yoshinobu; Taisei Hōkan (Return of Political Rule to the Emperor).
Meiji period (1868–1912)	
1868	Restoration of Imperial Rule; Meiji Restoration.
	Boshin Civil War (1868–69) begins.
	Charter Oath promulgated.
1869	Formal return of domainal registers to Emperor Meiji.
1871	Postal service established.
	Establishment of prefectural system.
1872	Railroad begins operation between Shimbashi and Yokohama.

大塩平八郎の乱 蛮社の獄	1837 Victoria becomes queen of England (1837–1901). ヴィクトリア英女王即位
水野忠邦、天保の改革	1839 Opium War begins in China (1839–42). 中国でアヘン戦争始まる
ペリー、浦賀に来航	
日米和親条約締結	
安政五箇国条約締結 安政の大獄始まる 桜田門外の変	1858 China signs Treaties of Tianjin. 中国、列国と天津条約を締結
薩長同盟が成立	1861 Civil War begins in the United States (1861–65). アメリカで南北戦争始まる
第2回長州征伐 大政奉還	1864 The First International is founded in London. ロンドンで第一インターナショナル結成
王政復古；明治維新 戊辰戦争始まる 五ヵ条の御誓文 版籍奉還	
	1870 Franco-Prussian War (1870–71) begins. 普仏戦争始まる
郵便開業 廃藩置県 新橋―横浜間に鉄道開通	1871 Unification of Germany. ドイツ帝国成立

	The Education Order is promulgated.
1873	Gregorian calendar adopted on 1 January (Meiji 5.12.3 according to the lunar calendar).
	Conscription Ordinance enacted.
	Land Tax Reform Law issued.
1874	Itagaki Taisuke and others submit the Tosa Memorial.
1876	Treaty of Kanghwa signed with Korea.
1877	Satsuma Rebellion; Saigō Takamori commits suicide.
1880	Formation of the League for Establishing a National Assembly.
	Public Assembly Ordinance issued to control the Freedom and People's Rights movement.
1881	Imperial rescript promises the promulgation of a constitution and the convening of a national assembly.
	Jiyūtō (Liberal Party) is formed.
1883	Completion of the Rokumeikan.
1887	Futabatei Shimei begins publication of *Ukigumo* (Drifting Clouds).
1889	Constitution of the Empire of Japan promulgated.
1890	Mori Ōgai publishes "Maihime" (The Dancing Girl).
	Imperial Rescript on Education distributed to all schools.
	First session of the Imperial Diet convened.
1894	Anglo-Japanese Commercial Treaty of 1894 signed; it abolishes extraterritoriality.
	Sino-Japanese War of 1894–1895 begins.
1895	Treaty of Shimonoseki signed.
	Tripartite Intervention.

学制発布

太陽暦採用

徴兵令公布

地租改正条例布告

板垣退助、民選議院設立
建白書提出

日朝修好条規締結

西南戦争、西郷隆盛自殺

国会期成同盟設立

集会条例制定；自由民権
運動弾圧

国会開設の勅諭

自由党結成

鹿鳴館落成

二葉亭四迷「浮雲」

大日本帝国憲法発布

森鷗外「舞姫」

教育勅語発布

第一回帝国議会

日英通商航海条約調印；
治外法権の撤廃に成功

日清戦争始まる

下関条約締結

三国干渉

1876	The first successful telephone transmission is achieved by Alexander Graham Bell. ベル、電話を発明
1883	Sino-French War (1883–85) begins. 清仏戦争始まる
1896	First modern Olympic Games held at Athens. アテネで第一回オリンピック大会

1900	*Myōjō* (Bright Star) begins publication under the editorship of Yosano Tekkan.
1902	Anglo-Japanese Alliance signed.
1904	Russo-Japanese War of 1904–1905 begins.
1905	Natsume Sōseki begins serialization of *Wagahai wa neko de aru* (*I Am a Cat*).
	Treaty of Portsmouth signed.
1906	Shimazaki Tōson publishes *Hakai* (*The Broken Commandment*).
1910	High Treason Incident.
	Annexation of Korea.
	Ishikawa Takuboku publishes *Ichiaku no suna* (*A Handful of Sand*).
1911	Treaties signed with the Western powers that restore tariff autonomy to Japan.
	Nishida Kitarō publishes *Zen no kenkyū* (*A Study of Good*).
Taishō period (1912–1926)	
1912	Death of Emperor Meiji; accession of Emperor Taishō.
	First Movement to Protect Constitutional Government founded.
1914	Japan enters World War I on the side of Great Britain and its allies.
1915	Japan presents China with its Twenty-One Demands for territorial and other concessions.
1918	Rice riots provoked by spiraling inflation.
1919	Arishima Takeo publishes the novel *Aru onna* (*A Certain Woman*).
1920	Japan Socialist League founded; the government orders it to dissolve in 1921.
1921	Shiga Naoya begins serialization of his masterwork, the novel *An'ya kōro* (*A Dark Night's Passing*).

与謝野鉄幹「明星」

日英同盟締結
日露戦争始まる
夏目漱石「吾輩は猫である」

ポーツマス条約調印
島崎藤村「破戒」

大逆事件
韓国併合
石川啄木「一握の砂」

関税自主権回復

西田幾多郎「善の研究」

明治天皇没;嘉仁親王践祚

憲政擁護運動始まる

第1次世界大戦に参戦

対華二十一カ条要求

米騒動
有島武郎「或る女」

日本社会主義同盟結成

志賀直哉「暗夜行路」

1900 Boxer Rebellion in China.
中国で義和団の乱

1912 Republic of China established
with Sun Yat-sen as president;
Emperor Puyi abdicates.
孫逸仙（孫文）中華民国樹
立、清朝皇帝溥儀退位

1914 World War I begins.
第1次世界大戦始まる

1917 October Revolution in Russia.
ロシア革命

1919 May Fourth Movement in China.
中国で五・四運動

	Prime Minister Hara Takashi assassinated.
1923	Tōkyō Earthquake of 1923.
1925	Enactment of the Peace Preservation Law of 1925.
	Universal Manhood Suffrage Law passed.
Shōwa period (1926–1989)	
1926	Death of Emperor Taishō; accession of Emperor Shōwa.
1927	Financial Crisis.
1928	Zhang Zuolin assassinated by Japanese army officers.
1930	Shōwa Depression (1930–35) begins.
1931	Manchurian Incident.
1932	May 15th Incident; Prime Minister Inukai Tsuyoshi assassinated.
1933	Japan withdraws from the League of Nations.
1936	February 26th Incident.
1937	Kawabata Yasunari publishes *Yukiguni* (*Snow Country*).
	Nanjing Massacre (1937–38).
1938	Passage of the National Mobilization Law.
1940	Tripartite Pact signed by Japan, Germany, and Italy.
1941	Soviet-Japanese Neutrality Pact signed.
	Japanese attack Pearl Harbor, the Malay Peninsula, and the Philippines; war declared against the United States, Great Britain, and the Netherlands; The Pacific War (1941–45) begins.
1945	Atomic bomb dropped on Hiroshima and Nagasaki.

原敬刺殺

関東大震災

治安維持法公布

普通選挙法成立

大正天皇崩御；裕仁親王践祚

金融恐慌

張作霖暗殺

昭和恐慌始まる

満州事変

五・一五事件；犬養毅暗殺

国際連盟脱退

二・二六事件

川端康成「雪国」

南京虐殺事件

国家総動員法成立

日独伊三国同盟調印

日ソ中立条約調印

日本軍、真珠湾、マレー半島、フィリッピン攻撃；日本、対米英蘭宣戦布告；太平洋戦争始まる

広島、長崎に原子爆弾

1927 Chiang Kai-shek sets up a Nationalist government.
蔣介石、中国国民政府樹立

Charles Lindbergh flies across the Atlantic Ocean.
リンドバーグ、大西洋横断飛行成功

1929 U.S. stock market crashes, Great Depression begins.
世界大恐慌始まる

1933 Adolf Hitler becomes chancellor of Germany.
ドイツにヒットラー政権成立

1939 World War II (1939–45) begins in Europe.
ヨーロッパで第二次世界大戦始まる

	Japan accepts the terms of the Potsdam Declaration.
	Occupation of Japan by the Allied Powers (1945–52).
	The breakup of industrial and financial combines.
1946	Implementation of the Land Reforms of 1946 begins.
	Constitution of Japan promulgated.
1947	Enactment of the Fundamental Law of Education.
	Dazai Osamu publishes the novel *Shayō* (*The Setting Sun*).
1949	Yukawa Hideki awarded the Nobel Prize for physics.
1951	San Francisco Peace Treaty and the first of the United States-Japan security treaties signed.
1953	Television broadcasting begins in Japan.
1954	Self Defense Forces established.
1956	Mishima Yukio publishes the novel *Kinkakuji* (*The Temple of the Golden Pavilion*).
	Soviet-Japanese Joint Declaration reestablishes diplomatic relations between the two countries.
	Japan granted membership of the United Nations.
1960	Second of the United States-Japan security treaties signed in Washington; demonstrators against ratification of the treaty besiege the Diet building.
1962	Abe Kōbō publishes the novel *Suna no onna* (*The Woman in the Dunes*).
1964	Eighteenth Summer Olympic Games (Tōkyō Olympic Games) held in Tōkyō.
1965	Korea-Japan Treaty of 1965 signed; diplomatic relations restored.

ポツダム宣言受諾	**1945** Harry Truman, Joseph Stalin, and Winston Churchill call for the unconditional surrender of Japan in the Potsdam Declaration. ポツダム宣言で日本に無条件降伏を もとめる
連合国軍、本土進駐	
財閥解体 農地改革施行	United Nations established. 国際連合成立
日本国憲法公布 教育基本法公布	
太宰治「斜陽」	
湯川秀樹、ノーベル物理学賞受賞	**1949** People's Republic of China established. 中華人民共和国成立
サンフランシスコ平和条約、日米安全保障条約調印	**1950** Korean War begins (1950–53). 朝鮮戦争始まる
テレビ放送開始	
自衛隊設立	
三島由紀夫「金閣寺」	
日ソ共同宣言調印	**1957** Soviet Union launches the first space satellite, Sputnik 1. ソ連、初の人工衛星スプートニク1号の打ち上げに成功
日本、国際連合に加盟	
日米新安全保障条約調印；安保闘争激化	
安部公房「砂の女」	**1962** Cuban missile crisis. キューバ危機
東京オリンピック開催	
日韓基本条約調印	**1966** Cultural Revolution sweeps across China. 中国で文化大革命

1968	University upheavals of 1968–69 begin.
	Ogasawara Islands returned to Japanese sovereignty by the United States.
1970	EXPO '70 opens in Ōsaka.
1972	Okinawa returned to Japanese sovereignty by the United States.
	China-Japan Joint Communiqué of 1972 issued; it announces the establishment of diplomatic relations.
1973	Oil crisis.
1976	Lockheed Scandal.
1978	New Tōkyō International Airport opens.
	China-Japan Peace and Friendship Treaty signed.
1987	Japanese Trade Union Confederation formed.
1988	Recruit Scandal.
Heisei period (1989–)	
1989	Death of Emperor Shōwa; accession of Emperor Akihito.
	Structural Impediments Initiative Talks between the United States and Japan begins.
1990	Formal enthronement of Emperor Akihito.

大学紛争激化

小笠原諸島返還

日本万国博覧会開催

沖縄祖国復帰

日中共同声明発表

石油危機

ロッキード事件

新東京国際空港開港

日中平和友好条約調印

連合発足

リクルート事件

昭和天皇崩御、明仁親王践祚

日米構造協議始まる

天皇明仁、即位の礼

1969 U.S. Apollo 11 spacecraft puts the first man on the moon.
アメリカのアポロ11号、月面着陸に成功

1975 North Vietnam achieves the unification of Vietnam.
ベトナム全土統一なる

1980 Iran-Iraq War commences (1980–88).
イラン・イラク戦争始まる

1986 Nuclear accident at Chernobyl in the Soviet Union.
ソ連チェルノブイリの原子力発電所で大事故

1989 Tiananmen Square Incident in China.
中国天安門事件

Berlin Wall demolished.
ベルリンの壁崩壊

1990 Persian Gulf War commences (1990–91).
湾岸戦争始まる

Reunification of Germany.
東西ドイツ統一

1991 Soviet Union dissolved.
ソビエト連邦解体

1992	Law on Cooperation in United Nations Peace-keeping Operations passed by the Diet.
1993	Non-LDP coalition government is formed.
1994	Political reform bills pass in the Diet.
	Ōe Kenzaburō awarded the Nobel Prize for literature.
1995	Kōbe Earthquake.

PKO協力法成立

非自民連立内閣成立

政治改革関連法案成立

大江健三郎、ノーベル文
学賞受賞

阪神大震災

日本語索引　Japanese Index

English Index 英語索引

英語で読む日本史
Japanese History: 11 Experts Reflect on the Past

1996年 4 月19日　　第 1 刷発行
1999年12月17日　　第16刷発行

編　著　　講談社インターナショナル株式会社

発行者　　野間佐和子

発行所　　講談社インターナショナル株式会社
　　　　　〒112-8652　東京都文京区音羽 1-17-14
　　　　　電話:03-3944-6493（編集部）
　　　　　　　　03-3944-6492（業務部・営業部）

印刷所　　大日本印刷株式会社

製本所　　大日本印刷株式会社

ISBN4-7700-2024-4

講談社バイリンガル・ブックス

英語で読んでも面白い!

- 楽しく読めて自然に英語が身に付くバイリンガル表記
- 実用から娯楽まで読者の興味に応える多彩なテーマ
- 重要単語、表現法がひと目で分かる段落対応レイアウト

46判変型 (113 x 188 mm) 仮製

1 英語で話す「日本」Q & A / Talking About Japan Q & A

講談社インターナショナル 編　　　　　　　　320ページ　ISBN 4-7700-2026-0

外国の人と話すとき、必ず出てくる話題は「日本」のこと。でも英語力よりも前に困るのは、日本について知らないことがいっぱいという事実です。政治、経済から文化までモヤモヤの知識をスッキリさせてくれる「日本再発見」の書。

2 日米比較 冠婚葬祭のマナー
Do It Right : Japanese & American Social Etiquette

ジェームス・M・バーダマン, 倫子・バーダマン 著　　　192ページ　ISBN 4-7700-2025-2

アメリカでは結婚式や葬式はどのように行われるのか?　お祝いや香典は?……そしてアメリカの人たちも、日本の事情を知りたがります。これだけあればもう困らない。日米冠婚葬祭マニュアル、バイリンガル版。

3 英語で折り紙 / Origami in English

山口 真 著　　　　　　　　　　　　　168ページ　ISBN 4-7700-2027-9

たった一枚の紙から無数の造形が生まれ出る……外国の人たちは、その面白さに目を見張ります。折るとき、英語で説明できるようにバイリンガルにしました。ホームステイ、留学、海外駐在に必携の一冊です。

4 英語で読む日本史 / Japanese History : 11 Experts Reflect on the Past

英文日本大事典 編　　　　　　　　　　232ページ　ISBN 4-7700-2024-4

11人の超一流ジャパノロジストたちが英語で書き下ろした日本全史。外国人の目から見た日本史はどういうものか、また日本の歴史事項を英語で何と表現するのか。新しい視点が想像力をかき立てます。

5 ベスト・オブ 宮沢賢治短編集 / The Tales of Miyazawa Kenji

宮沢賢治 著　ジョン・ベスター 訳　　　　　216ページ　ISBN 4-7700-2081-3

「注文の多い料理店」「どんぐりと山猫」「祭の晩」「鹿踊りのはじまり」「土神ときつね」「オツベルと象」「毒もみの好きな署長さん」「セロ弾きのゴーシュ」の代表作8編を精選。ジョン・ベスターの名訳でどうぞ。

6 「Japan」クリッピング　ワシントン・ポストが書いた「日本」
Views of Japan from The Washington Post Newsroom

東郷茂彦 著　　　　　　　　　　　　　　　264ページ　ISBN 4-7700-2023-6

アメリカの世論をリードするワシントン・ポストに書かれた「Japan」……政治、外交、経済、社会のジャンルで取り上げられた日本の姿を、国際ジャーナリストが解説し、その背後にある問題点を浮き彫りにする一冊。

7 マザー・グース　愛される唄70選
Mother Goose : 70 Nursery Rhymes

谷川俊太郎 訳　渡辺 茂 解説　　　　　　　　184ページ　ISBN 4-7700-2078-3

「マイ・フェア・レディ」や「お熱いのがお好き」という題名も、マザー・グースからの引用だったって、ご存じでしたか？ 英米人にとって必須教養であるこの童謡集を、詩人・谷川俊太郎の名訳と共にお楽しみください。

8 ニッポン見聞録　大好きな日本人に贈る新・開国論
Heisei Highs and Lows

トム・リード 著　　　　　　　　　　　　　　224ページ　ISBN 4-7700-2092-9

国際化の進む日本ですが、アメリカのジャーナリストが鋭い目と耳で浮き彫りにしたニッポンの姿は、驚くほど平穏でいとおしく、恥ずかしいくらい強欲で無知なものでした。トムが大好きな日本人へ贈る新・開国論。

9 ベスト・オブ 窓ぎわのトットちゃん
Best of Totto-chan : The Little Girl at the Window

黒柳徹子 著　ドロシー・ブリトン 訳　　　　　240ページ　ISBN 4-7700-2127-5

小学校一年生にして「退学」になったトットちゃんは、転校先の校長先生に「君は本当はいい子なんだよ」と温かい言葉のシャワーで励まされます……バイリンガル版で、あの空前の大ベストセラーの感動をもう一度！

10 銀河鉄道の夜 / Night Train to the Stars

宮沢賢治 著　ジョン・ベスター 訳　　　　　　184ページ　ISBN 4-7700-2131-3

賢治童話の中でも最も人気の高い「銀河鉄道の夜」は、賢治の宗教心と科学精神が反映された独特の世界 —— 天空、自然、大地がみごとに描かれ、光と音と動きに満ち溢れています。ジョバンニと一緒に銀河を旅してみませんか。

11 英語で話す「日本の謎」Q & A　外国人が聞きたがる100のWHY
100 Tough Questions for Japan

板坂 元 監修　　　　　　　　　　　　　　　248ページ　ISBN 4-7700-2091-0

なぜ、結婚式は教会で、葬式はお寺でなんてことができるの？ なぜ、大人までがマンガを読むの？ なぜ、時間とお金をかけてお茶を飲む練習をするの？ —— こんな外国人の問いをつきつめてゆくと、日本文化の核心が見えてきます。

12 英語で話す「日本の心」　和英辞典では引けないキーワード197
Keys to the Japanese Heart and Soul

英文日本大事典 編　　　　　　　　　　　　　328ページ　ISBN 4-7700-2082-1

一流のジャパノロジスト53人が解説した「日本の心」を知るためのキーワード集。「わび」「さび」「義理人情」「甘え」「根回し」「談合」「みそぎ」など、日本人特有な「心の動き」を外国人に説明するための強力なツールです。

13 アメリカ日常生活のマナー Q & A / Do As Americans Do

ジェームス・M・バーダマン，倫子・バーダマン 著　　264ページ　ISBN 4-7700-2128-3

"How do you do?" に "How do you do?" と答えてはいけないということを、ご存知でしたか？ 日本では当たり前と思われていたことがマナー違反だったのです。旅行で、駐在で、留学でアメリカに行く人必携のマナー集。

14 ニッポン不思議発見！ 日本文化を英語で語る50の名エッセイ集
Discover Japan: Words, Customs and Concepts

日本文化研究所 編　松本道弘 訳　　　　　　　　　　　272ページ　ISBN 4-7700-2142-9

絶望的な場合ですら、日本人は「そこをなんとか」という言葉を使って、相手に甘えようとする……こんな指摘をうけると、いかに日本人は独特なものの考え方をしているか分かります。あなたも「不思議」を発見してみませんか。

15 英語で日本料理 / 100 Recipes from Japanese Cooking

辻調理師専門学校　畑耕一郎、近藤一樹 著　　272ページ（カラー口絵16ページ）　ISBN 4-7700-2079-1

外国の人と親しくなる最高の手段は、日本料理をつくってあげること、そしてその作り方を教えてあげることです。代表的な日本料理100品の作り方を、外国の計量法も入れながら、バイリンガルで分かりやすく説明します。

16 まんが 日本昔ばなし / Once Upon a Time in Japan

川内彩友美 編　ラルフ・マッカーシー 訳　　　　　160ページ　ISBN 4-7700-2173-9

人気テレビシリーズ「まんが日本昔ばなし」から、「桃太郎」「金太郎」「一寸法師」など、より抜きの名作8話をラルフ・マッカーシーの名訳でお届けします。ホームステイなどでも役に立つ一冊です。

17 イラスト 日本まるごと事典 / Japan at a Glance

インターナショナル・インターンシップ・プログラムス 著　　256ページ（2色刷）　ISBN 4-7700-2080-5

1000点以上のイラストを使って日本のすべてを紹介 —— 自然、文化、社会はもちろんのこと、折り紙の折り方、着物の着方から、ナベで米を炊く方法や「あっちむいてホイ」の遊び方まで国際交流に必要な知識とノウハウを満載。

18 ビジュアル 英語で読む日本国憲法 / The Constitution of Japan

英文日本大百科事典 編　　　　　　　　　　　208ページ　ISBN 4-7700-2191-7

難しいと思っていた「日本国憲法」も、英語で読むと不思議とよく分かります。日本国憲法を、59点の写真を使って、バイリンガルで分かりやすく解説しました。条文中に出てくる難解な日本語には、ルビや説明がついています。

19 英語で話す「世界」Q & A / Talking About the World Q & A

講談社インターナショナル 編　　　　　　　　　320ページ　ISBN 4-7700-2006-6

今、世界にはいくつの国家があるか、ご存じですか？　対立をはらみながらも、急速に1つの運命共同体になっていく「世界」 —— 外国の人と話すとき知らなければならない「世界」に関する国際人必携の「常識集」です。

20 誤解される日本人 外国人がとまどう41の疑問
The Inscrutable Japanese

メリディアン・リソーシス・アソシエイツ 編　賀川洋 著　　　232ページ　ISBN 4-7700-2129-1

あなたのちょっとした仕草や表情が大きな誤解を招いているかもしれません。「日本人はどんなときに誤解を受けるのか？」そのメカニズムを解説し、「どのように外国人に説明すればよいか」最善の解決策を披露します。

21 英語で話す「アメリカ」Q & A / Talking About the USA-Q & A

賀川洋 著　　　　　　　　　　　　　　　　　312ページ　ISBN 4-7700-2005-8

仕事でも留学でも遊びでも、アメリカ人と交際するとき、知っておくと役に立つ「アメリカ小事典」。アメリカ人の精神と社会システムにポイントをおいた解説により、自然、歴史、政治、文化、そして人をバイリンガルで紹介します。

22 英語で話す「日本の文化」/ Japan as I See It

NHK国際放送局文化プロジェクト 編　ダン・ケニー 訳　　　　　208ページ　ISBN 4-7700-2197-6

金田一春彦、遠藤周作、梅原猛、平川祐弘、西堀栄三郎、鯖田豊之、野村万作、井上靖、小松左京、中根千枝の10人が、日本文化の「謎」を解く。NHKの国際放送で21の言語で放送され、分かりやすいと世界中で大好評。

23 ベスト・オブ・天声人語 / VOX POPULI, VOX DEI

朝日新聞論説委員室 著　朝日イブニングニュース 訳　　　　　288ページ　ISBN 4-7700-2166-6

「天声人語」は「朝日新聞」の名コラムというよりも、日本を代表するコラムです。香港返還、アムラー現象、たまごっち、マザー・テレサの死など、現代を読み解く傑作56編を、社会・世相、政治、スポーツなどのジャンル別に収録しました。

24 英語で話す「仏教」Q & A / Talking About Buddhism Q & A

高田佳人 著　ジェームス・M・バーダマン 訳　　　　　240ページ　ISBN 4-7700-2161-5

四十九日までに7回も法事をするのは、「亡くなった人が7回受ける裁判をこの世から応援するため」だということ、ご存じでしたか？　これだけは知っておきたい「仏教」に関することがらを、やさしい英語で説明できるようにした入門書です。

25 日本を創った100人 / 100 Japanese You Should Know

板坂 元 監修　英文日本大事典 編　　　　　240ページ　ISBN 4-7700-2159-3

混沌と激動を乗り越え築き上げられた現在の日本。その長い歴史の節目節目で大きな役割を果たした歴史上のキーパーソン100人を、超一流のジャパノロジストたちが解説。グローバルな大競争時代を迎えた今、彼らの生き方が大きな指針となります。

26 NHK「ニュースのキーワード」
NHK: Key Words in the News

NHK国際放送局「ニュースのキーワード」プロジェクト 編　　　　　232ページ　ISBN 4-7700-2342-1

日本で話題になっている時事問題を解説する、NHK国際放送の番組「ニュースのキーワード」から「総会屋」「日本版ビッグバン」「ダイオキシン」など、33のキーワードを収録しました。国際的観点からの解説が、現代の日本の姿を浮き彫りにします。

27 ドタンバのマナー / The Ultimate Guide to Etiquette in Japan

サトウサンペイ 著　　　　　240ページ（オールカラー）　ISBN 4-7700-2193-3

サンペイ流家元が自らしでかした「日常のヘマ」「海外でのヘマ」を一目で分かるようにマンガにした、フレッシュマンに贈る究極のマナー集。新社会人必読！知っていればすむことなのに、知らないために嫌われたり、憎まれてはかないません。

28 茶の本 / The Book of Tea

岡倉天心 著　千 宗室 序と跋　浅野 晃 訳　　　　　264ページ　ISBN 4-7700-2379-0

一碗の茶をすする、そのささやかで簡潔な行為の中に、偉大な精神が宿っている ── 茶道によせて、日本と東洋の精神文化の素晴らしさを明かし、アジアの理想が回復されることを英文で呼びかけた本書は、日本の心を英語で明かす不朽の名著。

29 まんが 日本昔ばなし 妖しのお話
Once Upon a Time in *Ghostly* Japan

川内彩友美 編　ラルフ・マッカーシー 訳　　　　　152ページ　ISBN 4-7700-2347-2

妖しく、怖く、心に響く昔ばなしの名作を英語で読む。人気テレビシリーズ「まんが日本昔ばなし」から、「鶴の恩返し」「雪女」「舌切り雀」「耳なし芳一」「分福茶釜」など8話を収録しました。

30 武士道 / BUSHIDO

新渡戸稲造 著　須知徳平 訳　　　　　　　　　312ページ　ISBN 4-7700-2402-9

「日本が生んだ最大の国際人」新渡戸博士が英語で著した世界的名著。「日本の精神文化を知る最良の書」として世界17ヵ国語に翻訳され、1世紀にわたって読みつがれてきた不滅の日本人論。国際人必読の1冊。

31 開国ノススメ　孤立化するニッポンへの問題提起
Open up, Japan!

アンドリュー・ホルバート 著　　　　　　　　208ページ　ISBN 4-7700-2348-0

欧米の高級紙誌で活躍する一流の国際ジャーナリストが、海外で問われることの多い、日本の政治・経済・社会システムの問題について「どのように説明すればよいか」のヒントを与えてくれます。

32 NHK「日本ひとくち歳時記」/ Around the Year in Japan

NHK国際放送局「日本一口事典」プロジェクト 編　　256ページ　ISBN 4-7700-2457-6

ひな祭り、七夕、運動会、年賀状など季節感あふれる32のキーワードから、日本文化を斬新な視点で、簡潔に分かりやすく解説します。21ヵ国語で放送中のNHK国際放送局が発見した「ニッポン」。

33 「縮み」志向の日本人 / Smaller is Better

李 御寧 著　　　　　　　　　　　　　　　200ページ　ISBN 4-7700-2445-2

一寸法師から、盆栽、箱庭、茶室、俳句にいたるまで、常に小さいものを求め、小さいものへ向かう「縮み志向」。言語・風俗・文化などが似ており、また日本文化にも影響を与えた韓国、その初代文化大臣を務めた著者によって発見された日本文化の本質。

34 イラスト 日米ジェスチャー事典
The Illustrated Handbook of American and Japanese Gestures

スティーブン・N・ウイリアムス 著　　　　　264ページ　ISBN 4-7700-2344-8

知らなかったではすまされない――。誤解を受け、国際問題や大騒動を引き起こしかねない、日本とアメリカのジェスチャーの違いを、ひと目で分かるイラストで解説します。言葉よりモノをいう780のジェスチャー。

35 英語で話す「雑学ニッポン」Q & A / Japan Trivia

素朴な疑問探究会 編　　　　　　　　　　　272ページ　ISBN 4-7700-2361-8

日本にいる外国人と飲んでいて、一番盛りあがる話はなんといっても、「ニッポンの謎」についての雑学です。「日本の女性は、なぜ下唇から口紅を塗るの?」「なぜ "鈴木" という名字が多いの?」など、外国人が疑問に思う「なぜ?」に答えます。

36 英語で話す日本ビジネス Q & A　ここが知りたい、日本のカイシャ
Frequently Asked Questions on Corporate Japan

米山司理、リチャード・ネイサン 著　　　　　320ページ　ISBN 4-7700-2165-8

「世界市場で高いシェアを誇る日本の会社は?」「日本で最も古い会社」「日本の企業の世界での実力」「世界に通用する名経営者は誰?」「郵便局は世界最大の銀行?」など、日本の会社の人と組織について日本人も詳しく知りたい情報満載!

37 英語で話す国際経済 Q & A　一目で分かるキーワード図解付き
A Bilingual Guide to the World Economy

日興リサーチセンター 著　　マーク・ショルツ 訳　　320ページ　ISBN 4-7700-2164-X

不安定な要素をかかえて流動する国際経済の複雑なメカニズムを、日本最良のシンクタンクのひとつ、日興リサーチセンターが、最新の情報をおりこみながら初心者にも分かるようにやさしく解説。

38 もう一つの母国、日本へ / Living in Two Countries

ドナルド・キーン 著　塩谷 紘 訳　　　　224ページ　ISBN 4-7700-2455-X

著者が生まれた国、アメリカと自分の精神を育ててくれた国、日本という2つの祖国の狭間に生きる著名なジャパノロジストが、日本への熱い思いを込めて語る、日本社会の独特の仕組みや日本人の風習についての痛烈な意見。

39 国際貢献 Q & A　世界で活躍する日本人
Japan's Contribution to the World

外務省大臣官房海外広報課 監修　　　　288ページ　ISBN 4-7700-2192-5

日本は、世界の平和の維持のため、経済の発展のため、地球環境の保護のためなどにさまざまな努力をしています。その全容を紹介する本書は、これらの活動に参加したい人々のための絶好のガイドブック。

40 英語で比べる「世界の常識」
Everyday Customs Around the World

足立恵子 著　　　　304ページ　ISBN 4-7700-2346-4

海外の情報が簡単に手に入るようになった現在でも、日常生活での文化や風習の違いは意外に知られていないもの。世界各国の独特の文化や風習に対する理解を深め比べることで日本の独自性を再確認する本書から、国際交流の本質が見えてきます。

41 代表的日本人 / Representative Men of Japan

内村鑑三 著　稲盛和夫 監訳　　　　272ページ　ISBN 4-7700-2401-0

西郷隆盛、上杉鷹山、二宮尊徳、中江藤樹、日蓮上人、誠実で情熱に溢れる5人の日本人。彼らの生涯を、著名なクリスチャン・内村鑑三が英文で世界に紹介した名著をバイリンガル化しました。

42 英語で話す「アメリカの謎」 Q & A
Though Questions About the USA-Q & A

リー・ハウエル 著　　　　224ページ　ISBN 4-7700-2349-9

さまざまな分野で日本と深い関わりを持つアメリカ。「なぜ、懲役236年などという長い刑期があるの？」「なぜ、離婚率が高いの？」「なぜ、社長の給料があんなに高いの？」など、近くて遠い国、アメリカのあらゆる「WHY？」に答えます。

43 「英国」おもしろ雑学事典
All You Wanted to Know About the U.K.

ジャイルズ・マリー 著　　　　240ページ　ISBN 4-7700-2487-8

「英国人とアメリカ人はどう違うの？」「英国料理はなぜあんなにマズイの？」など、英国のナゾから大英帝国の盛衰、産業革命についての文化的考察、政治や王室のシステムまで、英国のすべてに迫ります。

44 「ニューズウィーク」で読む日本経済
The Japanese Economy as Reported in *Newsweek*

沢田 博 編訳　　　　224ページ　ISBN 4-7700-2543-2

グローバルな視点と緻密な取材で定評のある『ニューズウィーク』誌の経済記事から日本経済を読み解く、これが本書のテーマです。アメリカの経済アナリストたちや政府高官の辛口の批判や提言から、日本の抱える問題点がはっきりと読みとれます。

45 バイリンガル日本史年表 / Chronology of Japanese History

英文日本大事典 編　　　　160ページ（2色刷）　ISBN 4-7700-2453-3

日本の歴史を英語で語る。意外に難しいこの問題を解く鍵は年表です。歴史的事項が簡単に引けてそれに対する英語が一目でわかります。さらにそれぞれの時代の解説や、天皇表・年号表なども収録。日本の歴史を語るキーワード集として活用できます。

46 「宮本武蔵」名場面集 / The Best Scenes from *Musashi*

吉川英治 著　チャールズ・テリー 訳　　　　　　　　336ページ　ISBN 4-7700-2482-7

武蔵は本能の赴くまま、悩み、もがき、猛り泣いて、その修羅道から救われるべき「道」をさがし求めた。その生命の記録は、あまりにも繊細に無気力に堕している今の日本人に強く訴えかけてくる。欧米でベストセラーとなり、18ヵ国語版が出版された吉川英治の代表作。

47 英語で「ちょっといい話」 スピーチにも使える222のエピソード
Bits & Pieces of Happiness

アーサー・F・レネハン 編　足立恵子 訳　　　　　　　208ページ　ISBN 4-7700-2596-3

「逆境」「年齢」「感謝」「ビジネス」「希望」「笑い」「知恵」など47項目のテーマを、短く機知に富んだエッセイ・逸話・ジョーク・ことわざの形式で鋭く描写。意味のある話をしたいときに、スピーチ原稿のヒントに、一日を明るくするために、実用的なアイデアが満載！

48 よりぬき 徒然草 / Selections from *Essays in Idleness*

兼好 著　ドナルド・キーン 訳　　　　　　　　　　272ページ　ISBN 4-7700-2590-4

日本随筆文学の代表作である『徒然草』全243段の中から132段を精選し、英訳と現代語訳をつけました。真摯な求道者であり、醒めた眼をもつ認識者でもあった兼好が、独自の思想・美意識によって、無常論・処世訓・人間論・恋愛論などを簡潔につづっています。

49 英語で話す「医療ハンドブック」 / Getting Medical Aid in English

東京海上記念診療所 監修　黒田基子 著　　　　　　336ページ　ISBN 4-7700-2345-6

海外で病気になったらどうしよう？── 本書では、小児科・内科・婦人科などの科目別に、さまざまな症状を想定した「会話」と「文章」を対訳形式で展開することによって、英語で話さなくても指で指すだけで医者や看護婦とコミュニケーションできるようになっています。

講談社バイリンガル・ブックス　（オン・カセット/オンCD）　英語で聞いても面白い！

📼印のタイトルは、英文テキスト部分を録音したカセット・テープが、また 💿 印のタイトルは英文テキスト部分を録音したCDが発売されています。
本との併用により聞く力・話す力を高め、実用的な英語が身につく格好のリスニング教材です。

バイリンガル書籍

対訳 英語で話す日本経済 Q & A
A Bilingual Guide to the Japanese Economy

NHK国際放送局経済プロジェクト・大和総研経済調査部 編　　　　ISBN 4-7700-1942-4
46判（128 x 188 mm）仮製　368ページ

NHK国際放送で好評を得た番組が本になりました。クイズと会話形式で楽しく読んでいくうちに、日本経済の仕組が分かり、同時に英語にも強くなっていきます。日本語と英語の対応がひと目で分かる編集上の工夫もいっぱい。

バイリンガル とってもかんたんマイレシピ
Stone Soup : Easy Japanese Home Cooking

渡辺節子 著　　　B5判変型（189 x 257 mm）仮製　256ページ　ISBN 4-7700-2061-9

手軽な日本の家庭料理、わが家の味160品目の作り方を、英語と日本語で紹介したクッキングブック。作り方や調理器具などのイラスト付き。カロリー計算・調理時間もひと目で分かります。

対訳 サザエさん（全12巻）
The Wonderful World of Sazae-san

長谷川町子 著　ジュールス・ヤング 訳

- 吹き出しの中にオリジナルの暖かい雰囲気を大切にした英語、コマの横に日本語がつく対訳形式
- お正月、こいのぼり、忘年会など日本独特の文化や習慣には、欄外に英語の解説つき

46判変型（113 x 188 mm）仮製

第 1 巻	170ページ	ISBN 4-7700-2075-9
第 2 巻	168ページ	ISBN 4-7700-2093-7
第 3 巻	198ページ	ISBN 4-7700-2094-5
第 4 巻	164ページ	ISBN 4-7700-2149-6
第 5 巻	176ページ	ISBN 4-7700-2150-X
第 6 巻	160ページ	ISBN 4-7700-2151-8
第 7 巻	168ページ	ISBN 4-7700-2152-6
第 8 巻	168ページ	ISBN 4-7700-2153-4
第 9 巻	172ページ	ISBN 4-7700-2154-2
第10巻	172ページ	ISBN 4-7700-2155-0
第11巻	176ページ	ISBN 4-7700-2156-9
第12巻	168ページ	ISBN 4-7700-2157-7
化粧箱入り全12巻セット		ISBN 4-7700-2435-5

対訳 OL進化論
Survival in the Office

秋月 りす 著

- 吹き出しに英語、そのコマ横に日本語を配した対訳形式
- 4コマ漫画で状況が明確に設定され、感情表現や相づちのうちかたがよくわかります
- OLたちの普段の会話から「生きた」英会話が学べます

46判変型（113 x 188 mm）仮製

第 1 巻	144ページ	ISBN 4-7700-2390-1
第 2 巻	144ページ	ISBN 4-7700-2501-7
第 3 巻	144ページ	ISBN 4-7700-2502-5

実用英語の総合シリーズ

- 旅行・留学からビジネスまで、コミュニケーションの現場で役立つ「実用性」

- ニューヨーク、ロンドンの各拠点での、ネイティブ・チェックにより保証される「信頼性」

- 英語の主要ジャンルを網羅し、目的に応じた本選びができる「総合性」

46判変型（113 x 188 mm）仮製

1 これを英語で言えますか?
学校で教えてくれない身近な英単語

講談社インターナショナル 編 　　　　232ページ　ISBN 4-7700-2132-1

「ブランコ、鉄棒、すべり台」「短縮ダイヤル」「○×式テスト」「$a^2 + b^3 = c^4$」「円の面積はπ掛ける半径の2乗」「いない、いない、ばー」…これらを英語で言えますか?　本書は日本人英語の盲点に77の分野から迫ります。

2 遠山顕の英会話・150のスパイス
ムリなく使える決まり文句

遠山　顕 著 　　　　　　　　　240ページ　ISBN 4-7700-2586-6
　　　　　　　　　　　 CD（70分×1）ISBN 4-7700-2587-4

「一杯いこうか?」「なるようになりますよ」「テコでも動きませんよ」など、欧米人の会話にもしばしば使われる決まり文句150を、"やさしい" "短い" をポイントに、選りすぐって紹介。すべて具体的な用例付きで応用も自由自在の、会話のスパイス集。(CD別売)

3 アメリカ旅行「使える」キーワード
場面別想定問答集

アンドリュー・ホルバート 著 　　　　240ページ　ISBN 4-7700-2481-9

出国から帰国まで、アメリカ旅行のすべてをカバーする一冊。ショッピングや食事、レンタカーの借り方からトラブル対処法まで、様々な状況で必要となる決め手のフレーズ。そんな「コトバ」と、初心者でも楽しく旅ができる実用的な「情報」を満載。

4 ダメ! その英語 [ビジネス編]
日本人英語NG集

連東孝子 著 　　　　　　　　　176ページ　ISBN 4-7700-2469-X

社長賞を貰ったアメリカ人の同僚に "You are lucky!" と言ってはダメ!?　ビジネスの場面を中心に、コミュニケーションの行き違い110例を紹介・解説。「この英語、なぜいけないの?」「この表現がどうして通じないの?」に答える、日本人英語のウィークポイント攻略本。

5 米語イディオム600
ELTで学ぶ使い分け&言い替え

バーバラ・ゲインズ 著　　　　　208ページ　ISBN 4-7700-2461-4

イディオムを使いこなせるかどうかが英会話上達の決め手! 本書は「勘定を払う」「仕事を探す」など、日常生活に即した80の場面別に600以上の重要イディオムを紹介。ただ機械的に暗記するのではなく、状況に応じた言い替え・使い分けがマスターできる。

6 どこまで使える? "go"と"come"
かんたん単語55の英会話

田崎清忠 著　　　　　　　　　208ページ　ISBN 4-7700-2527-0

"come" "take" "leave" など、中学校で習う初歩的な単語も、使い方次第で表現力が大幅アップ! 誰もが知っている簡単な単語55の意味と使い方を、肩の凝らないエッセイを通して紹介。つい見落としがちな、意味と用法の意外なバリエーションが気軽に学べる。

7 アメリカ留学日常語事典
これがなければ1日も過ごせない!

東 照二 著　　　　　　　　　192ページ　ISBN 4-7700-2470-3

アメリカのキャンパスには、独特の用語や表現がいっぱいあります。本書は、留学を志す人、アメリカのキャンパスで生活する人が知っていないと困る用語と情報を一挙にまとめて、日本人にわかりやすく解説しました。

8 マナー違反の英会話
英語にだって「敬語」があります

ジェームス・M・バーダマン、森本豊富 共著
　　　　　　　　　　　　　　208ページ　ISBN 4-7700-2520-3

英語にだって「敬語」はあります。「アメリカ人はフランクで開放的」と言われていますが、お互いを傷つけないように非常に気配りをしています。しかし親しい仲間うちで丁寧な英語表現ばかりを使っていては、打ち解けられません。英語にだってTPOがあります。場に応じた英語表現を使い分けましょう。

9 英語で「四字熟語」365
英語にするとこんなにカンタン!

松野守峰、N・ミナイ 共著　　　272ページ　ISBN 4-7700-2466-5

四字熟語をマスターし、その英語表現によってボキャブラリーも急増する一石二鳥のおトクな1冊! 日常よく使われる365の四字熟語を「努力・忍耐」「リーダーシップ」「チームワーク」「苦境」「性格」「能力」「友情」「恋愛」「宿命」などの意味別に分類し、英語にしました。